Controls in
Play Directing

CONTROLS IN PLAY DIRECTING

Types and Styles of Plays

Lawrence Carra
Professor Emeritus
Department of Drama
Carnegie-Mellon University

VANTAGE PRESS
New York / Washington / Atlanta
Los Angeles / Chicago

FIRST EDITION

Copyright © 1985 by Lawrence Carra

Published by Vantage Press, Inc.
516 West 34th Street, New York, New York 10001

Manufactured in the United States of America
ISBN: 0-533-06359-0

Library of Congress Catalog Card No.: 84—91275

To Marguerita

Contents

Preface   ix
Acknowledgment   xi
Introduction: Definition of Terms   xiii

Part 1. Type of Play
  1. Comedy   3
  2. Farce   30
  3. Tragedy   43
  4. Melodrama   54

Part 2. Style of Play
  5. Naturalism   71
     Realism and Selective Realism   83
  6. Classicism   90
     Neoclassicism   101
  7. Romanticism   104
     Neoromanticism   112
  8. Expressionism   118
  9. Surrealism   130
 10. Epic Realism   138
 11. Theatre of the Absurd   149
 12. Other Styles   159
     Impressionism   159
     Futurism   163
     Constructivism   165
     Happenings   168

Closing Statement   171

Bibliography   173
Index   175

Preface

In the Dean/Carra *Fundamentals of Play Directing* the major purpose is to discuss and present rudimentary techniques that give the director a base for operation in any form of theatre. Equivalent to the five-finger piano exercises in order to play the music without technical hindrances, the mastery of the fundamentals renders the staging of a play not an end in itself but a means toward bringing out its essential dramatic values.

But beyond mastering the fundamentals, we should also bear in mind that each play makes its own demands in interpretation. As much as we appreciate the absurdity of playing each piece of music with the same dynamics, so does the absurdity hold true for plays. However, it is not an uncommon experience to witness a play directed without any awareness of its uniqueness in type and style.

Controls in Play Directing applies the rudimentary techniques discussed in the *Fundamentals* to the different types and styles of plays. The characteristics are first analyzed before discussing the considerations that enter into acting techniques and overall directorial controls. Since the use of the terms *type* and *style* can vary widely, the first chapter defines these and other major theatrical terms as they are used in the context of the book.

No one play meets all the criteria set down for a particular type or style, nor can creative works be prescribed into neat categories. However, granted that the creative efforts of mature artists come first and rules follow, it has proven helpful to directors to have some point of reference for evaluating the specific play they are analyzing for production, and hopefully stimulate further creativity based on the dramatic values of the original, but without dependency on step-by-step analysis, set rules, or charts.

Unquestionably, there will be disagreement over some definitions and statements about terms, but if this study succeeds in helping the beginning director a little further forward in the ways of interpretation and in the ability to realize when something is going wrong, it will have served its purpose. The ability to do something about problems confronted in directing depends first on the recognition that problems exist.

In selecting play titles the tendency has been to refer to those with a longer history. The sources for the material used have been the extensive readings in the literature of art and drama, my own experience in seeing and analyzing hundreds of plays over years of teaching and directing, and class discussions with my students whom I wish to thank for their stimulating questions and criticisms.

L. C.

Acknowledgment

To Professor Alexander Dean, of the Department of Drama at Yale University, play directing was not necessarily either a divine or a mysterious gift, but an art in which, just as in other arts, certain principles could be both perceived and taught. Without belittling innate talent or claiming that an artist could be created where there was no inherent flair for the art, Dean believed that the knowledge and application of certain principles would avoid costly mistakes and eliminate economic and artistic waste.

Introduction: Definition of Terms

The artist enjoys the privilege of expressing himself without recourse to explanation or justification for the results. Whether the work, then, makes any impact on his contemporaries and the future is another matter. Unfortunately, the director cannot relish this benign state: his is the awkward task of having to interpret the work of art—in this case, the play—and to communicate his interpretation to others in the process of bringing the script to theatrical life on stage. Communication is apt to be easier and more accurate when a common language exists between the parties involved.

Wide variance exists in the meaning of many terms used in theatre arts. For a start, the vexed term *style* has several applications. We speak of the individual style of a writer, a painter, a composer, or a person's style of doing things. A man is congratulated for his style in dancing, meaning his gracefulness, finesse, and ease of moving; a lady dresses stylishly, meaning that she is dressed tastefully and fittingly in the latest fashion. We speak of period styles—Greek, Elizabethan, and Restoration—and find classic and Greek or romantic and Elizabethan often used interchangeably. Some say style when they intend genre or type of play; others apply the term only to outstanding plays of earlier periods. The same generalities exist in discussing types of plays: farces are called comedies; sentimental dramas, melodramas.

If it were only a matter of pedagogy, these generalizations in the use of terms could remain an academic matter for scholars to debate. But all too frequently they indicate a significant failure to understand the true meaning of a text, to recognize why the play is not coming together, and to distinguish period tastes and conventions from basic attitudes. Instances are common in the theatre where plays have failed because of the director's weakness in interpretation and execution in matters of genre, style, and such. A folk comedy is directed as a serious drama; a realistic French play of ideas is inundated in romantic acting and trappings; and of a serious melodrama, one critic is not certain whether "we are watching murder most foul or murder most funny."

It is important, then, that before undertaking these studies in directorial controls, we define the major terms used and analyze their relationship to each other in the process of transferring a script to stage life.

The type of play or genre in a direct sense defines the basic attitude that the writer assumes toward life. He may look at an event from a farcical, comic, tragical, or melodramatic point of view, or he may change his basic attitude and move from the comic to the tragic in the final scenes of his play. Or a writer may observe an event philosophically and see it as quite *absurd*; and he can express this absurdist world by juxtaposing farce and tragedy, as one approach among many. A play's type is not always this clear, but then these are the scripts that need special care and planning. Important to recognize is that the writer's basic attitude, besides underpinning the work, sets the tone of the play and creates its fundamental rhythm and mood. Genre, in summary, is the guide to the emotional control of the play through which we achieve tonal unity in all aspects of production.

The purpose behind the writing may be none other than to entertain the audience—a farce, for example, entertains by its hilarity; a melodrama, by its stress on suspense. But some authors may have a purpose beyond entertainment—jabbing the farce along may be the author's intent to ridicule or satirize, giving us the *satiric* farce or comedy; or the melodrama, driven hard by the author's prejudices, may attack the viciousness of society. By adding the author's purpose to the type of play we can list: *social* dramas, *thesis* plays, comedies of *manners*, *psychological* melodramas, and so on. If a play has a purpose beyond the obvious one of entertainment, we should recognize it in order to know the controls to exercise.

The elements of a play are the components by which we arrive at an understanding of the purpose behind the writing and the type or genre of play. We arrive at this through an analysis of the characters involved, the plot or action presented, the language used, the idea directly or indirectly expressed, the environment in which it takes place, and finally the overall dynamics and mood generated by the interplay of these components. We should recognize the fact, however, that the total experience of a play does not rest in these elements separately, nor in the manner in which they are structured—a play in totality is more than its parts.

Style is the manner of dramatic expression that the author chooses to use. The basic attitude in the writing may be *comic*, the purpose behind the writing may be *satiric*; but in choosing the manner of expressing the satiric comedy, the author may decide to do it either *realistically* or *romantically*, to cite two of the fundamental manners of dramatic expression. Style, then, is the author's manner of expressing the basic attitude. In these terms, *The Lady's Not for Burning*, by the twentieth century author Christopher Fry, is a *romantic* satiric comedy, while *Volpone*, by the seventeenth century Ben Jonson, is a *realistic* satiric comedy.

Both styles relate the plays to the world around us, regardless of the time when written or the period in which localized. As such, they are considered to be within the theatre of illusion. The theatre of illusion, however, when compared to our world, is actually highly selective, or romantic, classic, stylized, naturalistic, impressionistic, and so on. There are other plays that relate more specifically to the world of the mind and which in their fashion create a theatrical truth—a non-illusionary kind of theatre—that is expressionistic, or surrealistic, constructivistic, epic, and so on.

Ultimately, style becomes the controlling guide to the manner of acting, the design and use of setting, properties, costumes, lighting, and sound, and the controls of the fundamentals of directing. Style sets the limits within which all phases of production are unified.

Theatrical conventions refer to the conventions of a particular age that are directly operative on the structure of the play, the technique of acting, and the mechanics of staging. In the Elizabethan era, the conventions of direct communication with the audience and unlocalized areas in a flexible open stage had direct bearing on the structure of Shakespeare's plays, just as the conventions of our generally proscenium-oriented theatre with its stage machinery and instruments have their effect on contemporary playwriting. The staging of Maxwell Anderson's romantic tragedy *Elizabeth, the Queen* evolves out of our own theatrical conventions and not out of Shakespeare's, even though the play is about his contemporaries. Stylistically, *Elizabeth, the Queen* is a romantic work; but the conventions of acting and staging relate to the proscenium stage. Stylistically, Shakespeare's *Richard III* is also a romantic work; but in this case the conventions of acting and staging relate to the open stage of the Elizabethans. Yet, many are confused in accepting Shakespeare's dark comedy *Measure for Measure* within the sphere of realism because of this fact of differing theatrical conventions. The confusion here arises from associating the term *realism* only with contemporary conventions of staging and play structuring. The confusion in separating stylistic concepts from theatrical conventions becomes further aggravated when the term *classicism*, as a style of playwriting, is applied to plays as distinctive as Anouilh's *Antigone*, Miller's *A View from the Bridge*, and Sophocles' *Oedipus Rex*.

Period conventions, on the other hand, as distinguished from theatrical conventions, apply to the art, culture, modes, and manners of a period. In researching the background to *Elizabeth, the Queen* for authenticity and enrichment, we study the art and culture of the Elizabethan era to capture the spirit and flavor of the age; and also study the modes and manners of the time for ideas in handling costumes, duelling, social etiquette, and so on. Unquestionably, we must recognize the elements that distinguish style from theatrical conventions and these from period conventions, for only then can we see each part in proper perspective to the requirements of the play. A realistic nineteenth century sentimental comedy does not become a melodrama to be burlesqued because it uses the accepted asides, soliloquies, or tableaux of its day; nor does naturalistic detailing in acting and staging bog down a play of classic dimension like Miller's *A View from the Bridge;* nor do romantic struttings destroy an idealogical, realistic play like Camus' *Caligula,* set in the Roman period.

The connotative values[1] of composition, movement, and rhythm convey to an audience the emotional qualities inherent in a scene by a treatment of these based on the emotional effect of shapes (line, form, and mass), direction of movement (positive and negative), and rhythmic pattern.

Fundamental design[2] is a concept arrived at by determining the meaning of an act or an entire play and then interpreting this meaning in ground planning, composition, and movement patterns—all working together to express the idea symbolically in pictorial terms.

The scheme of production grows out of the director's concept of a play, which in turn relates to the play's meaning, basic attitude, and style, and defers to no barrier of theatrical convention or production. Often the scheme of production arises out of a visualization in movement of the fundamental design conceived for the play. Shakespeare's romantic comedy *As You Like It* can be realized through several *schemes* of production without subjecting it to artistic disservice. We can stage it in a replica of the open flexible stage of the Elizabethans; or place it within the confines of the proscenium stage with a *scheme* of wing and borders for the court and forest scenes. Without destroying its romanticism, we can give it equal life on a space stage enveloped by a cyclorama, with a rear projection of a romantic stylization of trees; or we can create a scheme of an enormous child's storybook standing upright with its pages serving as scenic cutouts turned by attendants for scene changes. We can conceive a scheme of a forest-in-movement as Rosalind and her companions penetrate deeper into the woods; or we can set the play on an arena stage with flying ribbons outlining the scenic elements. Short of gimmicks, a scheme of production can extend to the limits of a director's imagination, provided that on the interpretative level it sustains the values of the play. Certain plays do not permit a wide range of schemes: a naturalistic play in which physical surroundings and atmosphere give it substance, probably breathes its truest life in the fourth-wall tradition of the proscenium theatre that first nurtured it.

Approach to rehearsal is determined out of the intrinsic needs of the play—the rehearsal procedure in directing a contemporary comedy of ideas, highly selective in its realism, is quite different from that of directing a mystery thriller. One play may justify an extensive period of probing into a character's background, with visits to the actual environments alternating with periods of improvisation to enrich the actor's perception of his character; another may require preliminary discussions on the ideas advanced by the playwright followed by rehearsals on line emphasis. Some casts are put on their feet immediately to sketch in movements and business, and to establish space relations and external circumstances in order to give the actors a frame of reference for study; others may require concentrated study and intensive rehearsal of major critical scenes in the latter part of the play before work begins on the earlier scenes. Some styles of writing call for a particular approach to rehearsals, which in turn develops philosophical principles about the process of bringing these scripts to life on stage. We are not thinking here of the actor-director-writer collaboration in which performances are the outcome of a long process of improvisation, but of approaches more in line with the "method" or "Brechtian" influence that work more effectively when applied to the styles of writing that gave them conception.

Finally, we must temper our approach within the limitations of the company and the time available for rehearsals. Ensemble companies may extend their rehearsals over a period of months, but circumstances force some directors to rehearse within a prescribed time. Approach to rehearsals must also be tempered by the experience of the company's members, their amateur or professional standing, and the nature of the group—whether a resident professional company, a university theatre group, a community club, or a professional cast assembled specifically for the play.

The fundamental elements of directing furnish the means of conveying the intellectual and emotional qualities of a play. They are inherent elements of every play directed, but each play, according to the characteristics to be emphasized, makes its own demands on the control of each.

FUNDAMENTAL ELEMENTS OF DIRECTING[3]

Composition is the rational arrangement of people in a stage group through the use of emphasis, stability, sequence, and balance, to achieve an instinctively satisfying clarity and beauty. It is the structure, form, or design of the group. It is not, however, the meaning of the picture. Composition is capable of expressing the feeling, quality, and mood of the subject through line, form, mass, and color. It does not tell the story. It is the technique; not the conception.

Picturization is the visual interpretation of each moment in the play. It is the placing of characters in a locale that suggests their mental and emotional attitudes toward one another so that the dramatic nature of the situation will be conveyed to an audience without the use of dialogue or movement. It is the outer action, that, in turn, makes the audience understand, at times contrary to the dialogue, the inner meaning or subtext existing within and between characters. Whereas composition contributes the rational arrangement of technique and the mood of the subject, picturization contributes the meaning or thought to the stage group. In summary, picturization is the concept; composition, the technique.

Movement is the stage picture in action. It comprises the moments of picturization in their ever-changing aspects. Like composition, movement has both a technical value and a mood value. Movement, such as an exit or an entrance or the hiding of an object, is supplied by the author for the necessary action in the progression of the story. There are other movements, however, supplied by the director for character evaluation, emphasis, variety, and mood expression.

Business and pantomime are frequently used interchangeably. It is well to point out the distinction between the two and the relationship of each to properties.

Business means going through the motions of opening and closing doors, wrapping bundles, dialing a telephone, pounding a table, and making other movements, gestures, and reactions without dialogue or in synchronization with dialogue.

Pantomime is action without words. By action is meant a sequence of facial expressions, gestures, hand operations, and body positions and movements that, observed from life, is used imaginatively by the actor and director to tell something about the elements of character, situation, locale, and atmosphere of a play. If these elements are made clear without the use of dialogue, they are said to be dramatized by pantomime.

Rhythm is one of the most important elements in creating impressions and emotions. The reason for this rests for the most part on our powers of association. When again and again throughout life we find that the sensations of rhythm within us are the result of definite bodily and emotional excitements, we grow to associate the rhythms that happen outside us with definite inner emotions and impressions; and consequently, when we read a scene of emotional tension, we are able to sense its rhythm. Association, therefore, plays an important part in the relationship between rhythm and the resultant emotion. In technical terms, rhythm is an experience we receive when a sequence of impressions, auditory or visual, has been ordered into a recurrence of accented groups. This experience is marked by a willingness to adjust ourselves emotionally and muscularly so as to conform with the accented groups we see or hear. Dependent upon the intensity of the impressions our experience is expressed by degrees of emotional and muscular reaction ranging from pure inner feeling to bodily movement.

[1] For a detailed analysis of these terms, the student is referred to the Dean/Carra *Fundamentals of Play Directing*, 4th ed., 1980, published by Holt, Rinehart, and Winston.

[2] Ibid.

[3] For a detailed analysis of the following terms, the student is referred to the Dean/Carra *Fundamentals of Play Directing*, 4th ed., 1980, published by Holt, Rinehart, and Winston. Reprinted by permission of CBS Educational and Professional Publishing.

PART 1

Type of Play

The type of play or genre in a direct sense defines the basic attitude that the writer assumes toward life. He may look at an event from a farcical, comic, tragical, or melodramatic point of view, or he may change his basic attitude and move from the comic to the tragic in the final scenes of his play. Or a writer may observe an event philosophically and see it as quite *absurd*; and he can express this absurdist world by juxtaposing farce and tragedy, as one approach among many. A play's type is not always this clear, but then these are the scripts that need special care and planning. Important to recognize is that the writer's basic attitude, besides underpinning the work, sets the tone of the play and creates its fundamental rhythm and mood. Genre, in summary, is the guide to the emotional control of the play through which we achieve tonal unity in all aspects of production.

CHAPTER ONE

Comedy

Plays dealing with the laughable aspects of life are called comedies. Although many plays called comedies include scenes acceptable in tragedies, it is important for an analysis of directorial controls to maintain the traditional distinction between the two. With this in mind, the term comedy is applied to those plays that contain amusing situations rendered in a cheerful atmosphere, with a certain lightness of touch in the dialogue and character drawing. The characters are involved in the lighter conflicts of life and ultimately overcome all problems to the pleasure of those characters with whom the audience is in sympathy. But even holding to this traditional distinction, the ideas in comedies are oftentimes as profound as those in tragedies. The difference rests in the writer's point of view: comedy, as frequently stated, is a way of looking at life with the mind rather than feeling it with the passions. In contrast to tragedy, the response to comedy depends on keeping the audience objective to the events being enacted on stage so that the mind, rather than the deeper feelings of the audience, is stimulated. Once the intellect enters into play, it brings about a sense of detachment that removes the spectator emotionally from the characters and circumstances resulting in a lessening of emotional involvement. The degree of emotional involvement engendered may vary according to the particular comedy, but the overall audience response to comedy depends on detachment and not attachment as a requisite for laughter. Moliere says it tersely: "Comedy fosters the detached spirit of amused obervation." Since the approach to directing comedy is based on this understanding of detachment or the objective point of view, plays emotionally weighted like tragedies will be considered under the directorial controls for tragedy rather than comedy.

The difference in degree of an audience's emotional involvement in the world of comedy becomes evident when comparing a sentimental comedy like O'Neill's *Ah, Wilderness* with the highly sophisticated comedies of Noel Coward, Samuel Taylor, or Tom Stoppard. The reason is that in sentimental comedies the dominance of deeper emotions and feelings tends to disguise the playwright's manipulation of story, character, and language in achieving his effects. We should be sensitive to these subtleties of contrivance in comedy, for it is a clue to some of the controls.

Closely allied to an audience's emotional involvement is the amount of mental response required. There are high comedies of wit and brilliant repartee, of satire and ingenious ideas, which fascinate the audience's intellect, as against the low comedies of situation and multiple incidents where laughter is aroused by physical antics. A line with a double meaning effects more mental stimulation than a pun, and in turn a pun produces more mental response than the action of a merinque pie flung into the face of a matron. In directing comedy we should also be alert to the amount of mental response, for this, too, affects controls.

TYPES OF COMEDY

Appreciating the need for detachment, the degree of contrivance and emotional involvement, the amount of mental response, and the comic point of view that pervades the type of play called comedy—all working together to amuse an audience—we must now look further and analyze the major interest in the play. However, we must not disregard the realities of playwriting. Any play worth its name declares its own individuality and deserves to be interpreted on its own terms. All the more imperative, then, to understand the characteristics of the several types of comedy, so that a basis for judgment can be established.

Situation Comedy

This is unquestionably the most popular type. The story holds the audience's interest, amusing it by showing easily recognizable types of people engaged in fulfilling their needs and desires with an intriguing singleness of purpose. Usually, they are comedies of domesticity, based on the everyday and conventional episodes of readily understandable problems. Characterization is developed only insofar as it suits the requirements of the plot. Humor is primarily gained out of the situations and predicaments that develop, rather than out of character enrichment or lines of dialogue. The playwright's purpose is neither to satirize nor to make sport of the characters and incidents, which more often than not reflect the accepted mode of behavior of the day. When social problems do become part of the play's circumstances, as in Neil Simon's comedies on the "wage-earning" set, they are dealt with lightly. The list is long of plays that could be considered under this category. The many television situation comedies of the domestic variety offer a daily accessible source.

Sentimental Comedy

This class of plays strengthens the communication and relationship of character on character in an atmosphere imbued with warm feelings, and with a humor that is mellow, casual, half-wistful, and often humble in utterance. In O'Neill's *Ah, Wilderness* and Van Druten's *I Remember Mama*, the stronger focus on recognizable characters, and the circumstances enveloping them, charms us into their problems so that we not only sympathize, but to some degree empathize with them. These are plays of sentiment and romance—a type quite dominant in eighteenth century dramatic literature. Their strong mass appeal accounts for their continuing popularity in television soap operas, though in these more tears than laughter are in order. James M. Barrie's plays are particularly proficient in this type of comedy. The plays of Kelly and Sidney Howard, though pressuring the sober and commonplace in their portrayals, are considered his American equivalents.

High Comedy

This term is applied quite loosely to a range of plays peopled with the sophisticated side of society. It is also used interchangeably with *comedy of manners*. For a more exacting definition, distinction is drawn between these two types based on the larger interest in the play.

While the comedy of manners makes fun with and ridicules the follies of a people, high comedy creates its entertainment out of these follies by bringing together keen-minded, articulate, and sophisticated characters who indulge in cultured dialogue filled with witticisms. The characters of high comedy have a compulsion to show off intellectually, provoking laughter out of their exchanges. It is this masterly use of language that gives high comedy its unique distinction and provides the primary source of entertainment when the writer is at top form. The distinction is readily seen when comparing comedies of manners like Moliere's *School for Wives*, Goldsmith's *She Stoops to Conquer*, Maugham's *The Circle*, and Van Druten's *The Damask Cheek*, with high comedies like Congreve's *The Way of the World*, Wilde's *The Importance of Being Earnest*, Coward's *Design for Living*, and Stoppard's *Rosencrantz and Guildenstern Are Dead*. The language of high comedy is a design in compression and selection; at its purest, it is wit. The elegant phrase, the verbal wit, the epigram, stand so strongly on their own as manifestations of intellectual showmanship that they grace our social conversation beyond the theatre, even when quoted out of context.

An interesting sidelight about high comedy is that its world is peopled by individuals who "belong" and seem to have no connection with the necessities of existence. How they earn their living or occupy themselves never enters our thoughts. It is enough that they amuse us with their scintillating conversation.

Comedy of Manners

These plays hold up to ridicule the modes and manners of the fashionable life of a period to stimulate our laughter. The playwright's purpose is not to satirize severely but to comment by viewing his characters in some incongruous way or by portraying them under circumstances that bring out the absurdities demanded by the fads, fashions, and custom of an age. The writer attacks the pretentious surface conventions of behavior and communication, but not the necessities of living. Monsieur Jourdain in Moliere's *Le Bourgeois Gentilhomme* does not realize the ridiculous figure he is cutting in his awkward attempts to imitate the manners of a society to which he aspires. There is satire here, as there is in Sheridan's *School for Scandal* and *The Rivals*, but it is satire that comes out of character behavior. In works like Barrie's *The Admirable Crichton*, Philip Barry's *Philadelphia Story*, or Albee's *A Delicate Balance*, the ridicule and satire are even less direct. In these the author places his emphasis firmly on the prevalent mode of behavior to be dissected. These are plays that belong to and reflect, without significant distortion or exaggeration, the very essence of social behavior at the time of writing.

In comedies of manners, where greater attention is paid to character drawing, the principal characters exemplify specific traits or passions which account for the follies committed and which offset each other, as in Moliere's *Tartuffe*, where Tartuffe's hypocrisy feeds off Organ's gullibility. Or the Protagonist is a social deviant, as in Moliere's *The Misanthrope*, parodying his idiosyncrasies and exposing his foolish notions to the world. This emphasis on character traits can be made still more selective and dominant to render the comedy of humors of a Ben

Jonson—a selection and sharpening of traits taken from many kindred souls in society to create the idealized individual, the prototype, who serves the central purpose of the play. This prototype may differ from any to be met in actual society, but the dramatic distillation sharpens the audience's awareness of the social comment.

Satiric Comedy

This type takes its tone from the playwright who, revolted by the society in which he lives, lashes out with ridicule and mockery. The satire may be shaped in witty phrases, but it has teeth to it that can attack, gash, and expose. Satire can be sardonic without moral sense, pity, kindliness, or magnanimity, as in Duerrenmatt's *The Visit* and Ionesco's *Rhinoceros*, both of which, however, leave comedy for the grim world of grotesque drama. Though we find barbs of satire in comedies of manners, the true satirists (like Aristophanes, Shaw, and Anouilh) attack institutions and ideas—each in his own way. Where Aristophanes, for example, creates farcical and fanciful worlds to make his political stabs, Shaw attacks his own mundane world. He shatters conventional thinking and behavior by replacing the accepted mode of reasoning with his own reverse logic.

In satiric comedy, as in comedy of ideas, the playwright speaks through his characters. He manipulates them or pins them on the blackboard for instruction. No matter who may be speaking on whatever side of the issue under scrutiny, the voice of the author is heard behind the mask. For this reason, we can say that characters in satiric comedy have no psychology of their own, yet are most intellectual and eloquent. They have stature and breath of vision. Satire requires a deep recognition of the dilemmas of life not only from the playwright, but also from the audience, who must have the knowledge to recognize and enjoy what is being satirized. In a larger sense, then, satiric comedy is a comedy of ideas in which the characters are the spokemen for the writer's varying points of view about the issue under discussion. These playwrights dramatize the moral, religious, political, or philosophic dilemma of life, so that they can attack politically, morally, and institutionally—as do Aristophanes, Jonson, Moliere, Shaw, Durrenmatt, and Frisch; or philosophically and metaphysically—as do Pirandello, Giraudoux, Anouilh, and Ionesco.

Within this broad spectrum of satire is *black comedy*, which denies the distinction between comedy and tragedy by interlacing the one with the other. It creates a world where moral and social values are reversed. It manipulates its satire by making the perverse logical and emotionally acceptable, thereby assaulting the audience's sensibilities. Writers like Duerrenmatt, Ionesco, Arthur Kopit, and Joe Orton reflect the ways of society as through a warped mirror, where the distortion of values shocks the audience or provokes violent responses. These writers form part of the absurdist school, juxtaposing contrasting emotions, physicalizing metaphors, creating symbolic characters, and in some plays using language, normally condemned as obscene, quite fluently in the conversation.

Comedy of Ideas

This type of play gives deliberate expression of a playwright's viewpoint on pertinent matters of the day. It is an earnest dispute on the contemporary scene displaying a masterful control of language to disarm or enrage each member of the audience. Its attempt is to be provacative and intellectually stimulating, usually in an engaging atmosphere of gentility—a kind of dialectical comedy of manners. The characters are mouthpieces for the conflicting ideologies under surveillance, with no more dimension than is necessary to portray the popularly accepted notion of the people who express the respective views. It is a highly selective type with enough plot line to justify bringing together the conflicting viewpoints. Stoppard's *Travesties*, Behrman's *Rain from Heaven*, Shaw's *Getting Married*, and plays of J.B. Priestley are strongly representative of the genre.

DIRECTORIAL CONTROLS:
INTERPRETATION OF THE PLAY

The Essential Nature of Comedy

We have attempted to contrast the characteristics of one type of comedy against another in neat categories; in practice, of course, no one type barricades itself behind a single set of characteristics to the exclusion of others. Shakespeare's *Twelfth Night* not only is strong in plot lines—witness its main story and the subplot of Sir Toby and his cohorts—but also encompasses keen, sensitive characters with a mentality that is agile and alert, ready to animate a conversation with sparkling wit, as in the brilliantly conceived first meeting between Viola and Olivia. This romantic comedy also includes farcical scenes built out of bold physical actions like the sword encounter between Viola and Sir Andrew Aguecheek. Here is a play rich in character, situation, language, and wit, favoring no one element above another. Does this mean that the demand for interpretation and controls is lessened or that the text will play itself? Somehow there is many a slip between initial perception and final execution. It is the ability to evaluate the balance between story and character, intention of the language, and purpose behind the writing that adds another dimension to assist us in decisions about interpretation and controls.

In *Twelfth Night*, we should know how Shakespeare proportions the witticisms and the physical antics, and their weight in relation to the main love story, particularly when the Sir Toby–Maria intrigues could overshadow the tender love scenes if allowed to run rampant. In *Tartuffe*, we should appreciate Moliere's interplay between character traits to taunt the manners and pretensions of his society, for herein reside the leads to proportioning the controls in detailing a delicious moment of satire, underscoring certain lines of dialogue, and highlighting witty phrases. Ben Jonson's vicious attack on greed in *Volpone*—a bitter satire of humors—contains characteristics that demand evaluations and ultimately controls different from those exercised in Shaw's romp on heroics in *Arms and the Man*.

The true values in a play can be distorted by a director, not deliberately but through his failure to recognize its essential nature. It is not unusual to see a high comedy stripped of its essence and played as a comedy of situation bordering on farce, slashed with pratfalls and other antics which by overemphasis or inappropriateness obliterate the essential play of language.

Understanding Why Comedies Amuse Us

We have said that in its traditional distinction, comedy is a type of play meant to amuse an audience. It is a way of looking at life with the mind rather than feeling it with the passions. It creates a sense of detachment, an objectivity to events, as a necessary requirement for amusement and laughter. None of these statements, however, explains why we laugh.

If we follow the explanations proposed by philosophers like William Hazlitt and George Meredith, we laugh because we are the only creature that is "struck by the difference between what things are and what they ought to be"; we laugh from an ability to "observe our own follies and frailties." Both imply man's ability to evaluate, which involves a mental process. In analyzing comedy, therefore, we should recognize "the difference" and the "follies and frailities," and then proceed to the practical task of projecting these to the audience in a manner that makes them seem plausible, so that laughter is generated. These are tangible beginnings that furnish the director with valuable tools toward the search for reasons why comedies amuse an audience.

We have observed that preparation for response to comedy requires primarily an understanding of life. In order to laugh we must understand, or at least sense, the reason behind a character's behavior, whether in speech or action. By understanding the reason, we can then be "struck by the difference"—we can realize that an *incongruity* exists. Veteran performers offer these additional insights: the reason behind a

11

character's behavior must be obvious and the recognition of the difference immediate; and the degree of obviousness must be related to the audience's intelligence and alertness. In simple terms, the humor of sophisticated high comedy is lost on an audience of children.

The recognition of incongruity is basic to stimulating laughter. Incongruity means that the presentation of a relationship, an idea, an association, or an event is out of the norm of expectation. The outcome takes us by surprise: the twist or turn of events is different than anticipated. Incongruity, as in the following observation by Louis Kronenberger, is expected behavior pitted against the frailties of human nature: "Here is the celebrated philosopher cursing the universe because he has mislaid a book."

Though the psychological motivation to laughter rests in the recognition of the incongruity, the milieu that nourishes the sting varies: it may be a mental picture, or the double meaning or sound of certain words; or it may rest in the interplay between character and situation, as in Sheridan's *The Rivals*, where we recognize the incongruity between what Mrs. Malaprop means and what she actually says, provided that the motivation for the intrusions—her pretensions to knowledge—is clearly defined. The comic actor Alec Guinness has said that: "In creating a comic character, it's the little touches, the subtle nuances, that make the difference. One takes a fairly ordinary character and plays him slightly out of frame, like the mad criminal I played in *The Lady Killers*—it's in the incongruity between that man's actions and reactions and a normal man's actions and reactions that the humor lies. In any event, I know what comic acting isn't—it isn't arm-waving and ranting and stomping about. Playing comedy is a much subtler art than most audiences or, indeed, most actors realize."

Coupled with the idea of incongruity as a provoker of laughter is the ability to recognize the immediate catalyst to laughter. This may be the *imitation* or *repetition* of a tone of voice or a gesture of hand; or the *release of tension* by the intrusion of an innocuous word or action; or an *anticlimax*, a favorite used by comedians, such as introducing an act or a personality with a great buildup and having it followed immediately by the ridiculous or the commonplace. Anticlimax is a *contrast* to the expected—the twist to the norm of expectation. In this regard, witticisms provoke laughter with their refreshing turn of phrase to the expected mode. Whatever the motivation, provocation, or stimulant to laughter may be, the director must know what it is and what to do about it.

Mentioned earlier is the statement that a degree of detachment to the events is an essential requirement for laughter. But this must be understood in its proper perspective. A cool, detached audience is death to comedy. For comedy to prosper, there must be warmth, comfort, and a compassionate rapport with the actors. To charm and win over an audience calls for ingratiating personalities on stage and the full resources of showmanship. What makes us amused at comedies rests not only with the text and its performance, but equally with the kind of rapport and environment that exists between audience and performance.

Performance Values

If the director is ignorant of the play's essential character and directs it within his limited understanding, misinterpretation and misdirection are bound to follow. The long history of comic performance bears this out: the experienced comedian knows that playing broadly for the belly laugh throws the interest on him (and to the detriment of the text). "Hamming" a role achieves the same results, to the despair of fellow actors, director, and writer, who watch the play "go out the window" while the actor bloats his egocentric performance out of proportion to the demands of the text.

Each play must be judged for what it is and directed accordingly to bring out its fullest dramatic values. If high comedy places more interest on the wit of a line or the clever turning of a phrase, does not this have a bearing on which lines of dialogue to point up and how to point them up? Subtlety and

13

restraint in acting, brilliancy and clarity in delivery, projection of an intelligence behind the delivery—all become values to work toward in rehearsals. And what of the actor's attitude toward his character and the tone of his performance? Oscar Wilde's high comedy *The Importance of Being Earnest* is endowed with charming, intelligent characters, witty dialogue, and satiric twists in language that defy conventional modes of thought and behavior. The actor is presented with a delicate challenge in acting and with problems different from the ones in a sentimental comedy. Granted that the actor must always project sincerity, in high comedy he faces the challenge of balancing his portrayal of character between deep emotional involvement and "playing the game." If it is to be otherwise, and the social manners and the code of ethics are something to be striven toward by the character, then a different level of culture is created. He is no longer a character in a high comedy, but the "cultured" equivalent of the two country girls in Moliere's satiric farce of manners, *The Affected Young Ladies*, where they are the butt of ridicule because of their stupidity. High comedy characters, however, are not stupid—they are alert and knowledgeable. Gwendolyn's insistence that Earnest propose to her is a conscious effort by Wilde to comment on this normally accepted social mode of behavior. The actors' task is twofold: to make us realize the characters' true love and at the same time show their enjoyment in "playing the game" of lovemaking in the socially accepted mode. Gwendolyn's thought might follow this line of reasoning: "Yes, I love you deeply, Earnest. You know it and I know it, but let's have the fun of you proposing to me as society expects." And Earnest, with the same intelligent awareness, goes through with the proposal. He "carries it off" beautifully, playing to the hilt.

"Playing the game" does not mean playing without sincerity. The audience must at all times be assured that the events are happening to real people. The characters must be founded in truth even though the playwright has singled out only certain aspects in his portraiture. It is in the nature of comedy writing, particularly high comedy, to create finely etched characters delineated out of carefully selected traits, but this does not mean that the actor discards sincerity and credibility in his portrayal of the role: actions and reactions are not exaggerated, they are heightened; insults are delivered with charm and grace; characters are involved in their problems and predicaments, but their involvement is less intense and penetrating, and therefore more resilient to stresses and strains. The energy is not to shatter, but to keep all on the bounce. The difficulty with this *objective involvement* demanded of the actor is that the inexperienced can fall easily into the trap of "playing at being funny." It is here that the director must be a sensitive receptor and rehearse the cast diligently for truth in performance. Nothing destroys credibility faster than an audience catching the actor *outside* his character. Comedy playing demands great technical proficiency, but the irony of it is that the technique cannot show. We expect the actor to be fully involved in his character and to play with conviction, and yet be sufficiently aware of the audience to hold for laughs. For the audience, no less is expected of them: we want them to be engrossed in the play, but not so emotionally immersed to suffer with the character when he is hurt, physically or spiritually. The challenge lies in this dilemma: the relationship between actor and character, actor and audience, and audience and the play. Part of the answer is in the theatre's fiction of reality—in the world of make-believe, we *choose* to believe it as real. The other part of the answer is in the actor's control of his role and in the director's control of the play.

DIRECTORIAL CONTROLS:
FUNDAMENTAL ELEMENTS OF DIRECTING

Regardless of style, the approach to directing comedy is guided by the need to keep both actor and audience in a degree of detachment to the role and the play.

Composition

Composition becomes one of the important aids toward bringing about this state of detachment. Rather than picturizing the storytelling and emotional relationships of character to character within a scene, compositional treatment, void of strong picturization, diminishes its emotional content. The actors play in opened-up body positions, relating more toward the audience than to themselves. Characters are composed primarily to draw the audience's eye to the principals participating significantly in a scene.

Knowledge of the type of comedy helps determine how strongly to compose for mood values, whether to have the audience be more attentive intellectually, as for high or satiric comedies, or respond more sensitively, as for a sentimental comedy. In general, the aim is to lessen the emotional projection of scenes through visual means—a control, however, that must not draw attention. Ease and subtlety are in order as the focus shifts from one point of interest to another.

Compositional control also maintains the tone of the comedy. The elegance in a drawing room comedy of manners rests as much in the balance and harmony of the composition of the characters as in the bearing of the actors.

Picturization

Picturization is confined to the two or three characters more directly involved in an action, and not extended to include the entire stage picture. The objective, as in composition, is to lessen the emotional content of a scene. In scenes where story values are important, picturization is used judicially to enrich these moments, but characters subsidiary to the action are kept visually neutral and composed to bring focus rather than to contribute emotionally. They remain attentive and related but not overtly expressive to the central action. The basis of control is to subordinate picturization to the lines of dialogue, and not have it dominate the text by heightened, extended, or intensified actions or pictures.

Movement

Movement in comedy, though always motivated, is often created out of technical considerations: drawing attention to the speaker, emphasizing a line of dialogue, stimulating visual interest, adding variety, and so on. Because its use is so particularized, it must be clearly and simply executed, besides being motivated. For the speaking character, the motivation to move can spring from his desire to convince others, thus justifying a move toward a character. Or, if the character delivers a witty phrase, the impulse for movement comes from the intent of the line and the character's desire (and the actor's) to point up the line for a laugh. Where movement is needed for variety to break up a long speech, the director can introduce business as motivation. Many movements in the higher comedies are justified by business no more complicated than a character taking a pencil from his pocket to point up a thought, then moving to a table and tossing it down as he points up another thought. Discursive scenes devoid of strong emotions and conflicts are most challenging in this respect, for though we can appreciate this technical application of movement as a means of delineation and stimulation, especially when confronted with the physiological and psychological fact that an audience's span of attention is limited, it still remains artistically unacceptable unless its use is motivated and related to the needs of text and character.

Business

Business can be divided into two categories: that required by the characters and the nature of the situation, and that created out of technical considerations. Either way, the search for business is not confined solely to the text. Especially in plays of manners, research into the culture of the age—beliefs, ways of living, and attitudes—can inspire a store of ideas for enriching character and situation. In high comedy, where language is of prime importance, business is reduced to its minimum and used essentially to underscore lines. However, business required by situation and character is usually defined in the text—a character puts on a jacket, opens a window, pounds the table, hands over a letter, puts on eyeglasses, and so on.

The line of distinction in the use of business in comedy rests in the appreciation of why it is there and how it is to be executed. If business is there to bolster the significance of a line, it is handled without embellishment so as not to call attention to itself. However, if the business, like putting on eyeglasses, is there to enrich character, then we might have the character fumble for the glasses, wipe them carefully, and adjust them slowly to his eyes before arranging the material to be read. The first control points up the line, the other delineates character.

Arbitrary considerations for use of business frequently come up in opening scenes where actions are at parallel: characters are introduced, circumstances set up, and issues, not yet in conflict, discussed. Talky and transitional scenes that introduce new characters and changes of circumstances come under this category. Normally, the playwright sets up these scenes in functions that permit a great amount of business. Functions like social gatherings offer opportunities for business to bring the emphasis where needed.

DEMONSTRATION

The setting, a drawing room. The function, a social hour with cocktails. The action, the host leads a discussion that involves several characters. Although business is introduced arbitrarily, the object is to motivate its use.

The host is seated when he picks up the discussion. His motivation to rise is justified; he moves toward the bar to replenish drinks. On his way over, he stops to deliver a line or two of dialogue to one of the characters, thereby pointing up the line; on the reaction he continues his cross and fixes drinks while the center of interest shifts elsewhere. The emphasis returns to the host for an off-

hand but important remark as he steps forward, stirring the beaker of liquor. Next, he serves the drinks, passing from one character to another, and each time pointing up a part of his argument that has special significance to the character he is with at the moment. Serving drinks becomes sufficient reason to move.

Throughout the movements of the host emphasis has remained on the conversation. By careful analysis of the text to note the order of speaking, and by the proper positioning of the characters in a diversified composition, each move, each relationship, and each bit of pointing becomes *the logical thing to do.* Justification for the business and movement makes it appear logical.

Atmosphere and Mood

Although the terms atmosphere and mood are often interchangeable and the demarcation from one to the other difficult to establish, the director should distinguish between the two. If we consider *mood* to be the sum of those dispositions that create the dominant emotional force affecting a state of mind, then mood is a result, while *atmosphere* can be compared to a fundamental element of directing equivalent to business. But where business is worked through character, atmosphere exists whether the director works for it or not. Ultimately a surrounding is clean, chic, barren, formal, unsightly, dirty, poverty-stricken, warm, close, cold, and so on by the arrangement, color, and details of its parts. These atmospheric touches, when particularized to a locale, can create planned moods to underscore the quality of a scene giving rise to feelings that are sad, cheerful, heavy, pleasant, haunting, pathetic, mournful, soothing, and so on.

Atmospheres such as time and weather conditions—a hot evening, a cold, rainy morning, a bright, sunny afternoon—are also conducive to affecting feelings by the mood they create. Sound and lighting effects can also contribute their share in projecting these atmospheres, but, when circumstances warrant, there is opportunity to enrich scenes through character business: moving slowly, fanning, wiping brows, removing or putting on garments, rubbing hands, etc. Selection and arrangement of furniture also projects a specific atmosphere through its line, form, mass, and positioning. However, mood and atmospheric touches for the purpose of toning should remain subordinate, unless their use in the text brings out a meaning as clearly as a line of dialogue. Flooding a scene with atmospheric details can shift the values to moods and feelings rather than to the conversation which, though set off by the atmosphere, should remain uppermost. The cool, calm evening in Shaw's *Heartbreak House* should be bright and lightly colored, and not redolent with moonlight and multiple shadows, if the audience is to be attentive and not sit in partial reverie through long periods of discussion.

Rhythm

Rhythm is the most sensitive area of control in directing comedy. Since the emotional character of comedy is inherently light and fluctuating, and partially dependent on interaction between it and the audience, decisions based on technical needs often dictate the dynamics of rhythm.

In comedy much is said about pacing, which to some often means fast tempo. Unfortunately, playing for fast tempo can diffuse understanding when language carries the meaning of a scene. Pace comes from a forward movement that is sustained by the immediate pickup of cues as one of several controls. However, this does not mean fast delivery which can blur meaning as drastically as ineffectual delivery. Comedy calls for a rhythm that is easy-flowing and effortless. This is achieved by working at pace through other means than a fast tempo in action or delivery, without disregarding the fact that tempo is an inseparable component of the ultimate rhythmic impression.

The qualities to strive for are brilliancy and effervescence, both of which are basic to the spirit of comedy playing. These exist only when projected by the actor who delivers a line with crystalline articulation and proper enunciation. Scenes must also be kept bouncing by lifting the endings of lines. Through these disciplines—combined with the pickup of cues, proper phrasing within a scene, building toward minor climaxes, and shifts in tempo to give variety to the dynamics—the pace of a scene is kept vibrant and exciting.

Variety of tempo in scene playing is an effective way to maintain the forward movement and the lift in vitality necessary to the spirit of comedy. Each scene needs special attention to discover its right tempo. Indications may be found in the type of characters, the tension of the scene, and the locale and circumstances; but even here the justification for tempo variations needs to be considered from a technical point of view when scenes that are neutral or devoid of inner dynamics follow one another. If an unhurried narrative precedes a scene, the tempo of the subsequent scene can be accelerated by infusing it with some urgency appropriate to the occasion: the character is on his way out, he is fired up by his convictions, or a visitor is expected; or if the content offers no grounds for this kind of interpretation and a quickening of pace is essential, the solution may be found in telescoping transitional lines, breaking up the scene through movement, and other similar technical controls.

OTHER CONSIDERATIONS IN DIRECTING COMEDY

Playing Serious Scenes in Comedy

Serious scenes in comedy must be modified in their emotional intensity to keep them within the underlying comic spirit. Fundamentally, the types of comedies discussed above differ from drama or tragedy by the sense of humor that runs through them. A sudden shift from this humor to heavy emotional commitment can break the rapport established between play and audience, and catching the audience unprepared can often result in unwanted laughter. But comedies do have their

21

serious moments and their love scenes. The love scenes are not difficult to control, since the writer never develops them to a degree that stalls the main action. As contributive scenes they are played lightly in acting, toning, and picturization. Played otherwise for languor and soft sentiment, or romanticized, love scenes can slow down the pace. The problem of control is increased for serious scenes. The emotional intensity in acting must be toned down and the visual aspects of the scene treated compositionally rather than picturized in depth. The transitions into and out of serious scenes require special attention since these are the moments that blend them into the tonality of the comedy. How exactly are these transitions handled? The answer involves an analysis of controls used in deepening or lightening an emotional moment.

DEMONSTRATION

Scene: Trofimov's entrance in Act I *of Chekhov's* The Cherry Orchard.

Trofimov enters unexpectedly to pay his respects to Lyubov, who has just arrived home after a long absence and at the moment is in high spirits. On his entrance, the scene takes on a serious tone.

The emotional coloring in the characters' reactions and delivery of lines tells the audience that Trofimov revives memories of a tragic happening. The picturization of the scene can be composed to accentuate the deeper feelings of the characters related to the basic situation. The inner process of thoughts and feelings is given extension. For more intensification, Lyubov, unable to contain her tears after embracing Trofimov, moves to the couch near her and collapses. After a moment she moans, "My Grisha, my little boy . . . Oh, Grisha, my son." She gives way to her emotions as Varya bends over to comfort her; stirred by the brutality of her fate, Lyubov laments: "My little boy was lost . . . drowned." Then, in full grip of defiance, cries out: "Why?"

The emotional impact can be further accentuated compositionally by grouping the characters into a form that draws the lines inward, principally through weak body positions. Negative use of movement is made in Lyubov's approach and collapse, and in Varya's cross. By these controls in acting and staging the audience's empathy is strengthened.

However, if instead of picturizing this extensively, the four characters are held in an arbitrary composition with Lyubov and Trofimov sharing the scene while the others focus on them, the action assumes a tone suitable to comedy where feelings are in a lighter vein.

In the first method we picturize for deep emotional response; in the second we compose arbitrarily for more audience detachment. The compositional treatment lessens the emotional content of the scene—provided that there is also a change in dynamics from the comic to the serious, and in the emotional commitment of the actor.

For the transition from the serious to the comic, Chekhov allows for the adjustment by having Lyubov leave her area of grief in moving toward the exit. It is on this move that she comes out of herself and notices Gaev. Chekhov has relieved the earlier emotion by going from inward reflection to outward observation. For the first time since her arrival, which was filled with feelings of warmth and joy, Lyubov becomes conscious of life's decay—Gaev's aging features and Pishchik's gout. Technically, Lyubov's highly emotional scene on the entrance of Trofimov is relieved by the following steps in preparation for the lighter mood: change in area playing, use of positive movements in the cross to a strong area, and use of greater amount of movement (Lyubov's cross, Gaev's cross to Lyubov, Pishchik's rise from the chair).

Illuminating the Comic Text

Comedy Acting

In the words of G. B. Shaw: "Comedy requires a special technique of acting—great virtuosity in sudden transitions from one thought, one attitude to the next. This is fully accomplished acting, for there is no other sort of acting except *bad* acting—acting within which the actor relishes himself in his emotions and imagination rather than in the requirements of the text where the exercise is in the skill of projecting the scene requirements."

The implications are clear: comedy is a hard taskmaster demanding that the actor carry his truth in his technique. "An experienced actor has an outside eye," says Lynn Fontanne, "you can look at yourself; and an outside ear that tells you it is the wrong inflection." Yet comedy playing permits no externalization, for an audience is not prone to be amused when it catches the actor at work with the mechanics of control—a bit of timing, a lifted phrase, or a calculated gesture. The magic will have disappeared, as it does with clumsy sleight of hand. The hope for achievement rests in comedy's own truth: mastery of technique, first through knowledge and then through exercise, which in turn permits the actor to free his inspiration and act with truth.

The demand for mastery of technique is no different from any other art except for the problem that is the bugaboo, more real than imagined, of all actors: his own instrument. Directors must be aware of this and be sensitive to the difference. A director can be helpful in instilling confidence if he is secure about the text (its meaning and objectives), exacting in communicating these, knowledgeable of the techniques to be mastered, sympathetic with suggestions from the actors, and patient in waiting for results.

The Laugh Lines

These are the blocks that build the edifice of the comic spirit. Among the tasks in preparing the script for production is the one of identifying laugh lines and noting the reason behind their humor. The first tells us the lines to point up in performance; the second, the inflection, gesture, volume, and the amount and kind of business to use. The laugh comes from the immediate meaning within the line, or from gesture that projects meaning like the line of dialogue. But the ultimate meaning may depend on the preceding feed lines, even though understanding the nature of the total situation is often enough. "Getting a laugh" needs preparation and understanding, as well as technique in pointing and delivery. Let us look at these in detail.

1. Preparation, Understanding, and the Audience

Playwright, actors, director, and audience carry their individual responsibilities in these areas, but the burden of responsibility rests with the workers on the stage side. This can be readily demonstrated through a period play like Moliere's *The Affected Young Ladies*, where the humor from the satire also depends on an audience's understanding.

An inherent nature of comedy is its topicality. In comedies, past or present, where the patterns of behavior are universal in appeal, the impact on the audience is immediate. On the other hand, personalities, events, locales, and the like are often mentioned that have lost significance because their special reference had meaning only at the time of writing. These references should be amended to have meaning for a present audience, or else cut. In contrast to this are the topicalities—the manners and fashions of a period satirized by a comic writer like Moliere—which can have meaning for a contemporary audience provided they are emphasized in correct perspective before the occurrence of the scenes where sport is made with them. An example of this is the opening scene of *The Affected Young Ladies*. Even without prior knowledge of the affectation under ridicule, the audience gains the necessary background in the scene between the two gentlemen, provided the important lines are pointed and the gentlemen portray their roles in strict obedience to the proper mode of behavior. Satire depends on the assumption that the audience fully understands the normal behavior of whatever is being satirized. A director's responsibility is to know the normalcy of behavior and to focus attention on it, so that later, the diversions become ludicrous because they are *out of norm*.

2. Technique in Pointing and Delivery

An actor's sense of timing may or may not be an inborn asset, but only long exposure in performance develops the acute sensitivity to audience response which is an integral part of timing. Timing in itself, however, is meaningless unless other factors of control work together harmoniously. The control in delivery considers the following:

(a) The plant or feed lines are carefully rendered and emphasized. Fontanne and Lunt say: "You have to make your feed line clear, in order that the other person tops you, and so that the funny line gets the laugh."

(b) To intensify the contrast or incongruity, the tone that best expresses the humor is employed. Should the tone be in imitation or exaggeration? Should it be nasal, aspirate, dry, drawl, and so on? Oftentimes, in certain characterizations the delivery of a line with an unusual tone of voice helps project its humor; also the contrast or incongruity between thought and delivery, e.g., shouting: "Quiet! The baby's asleep!"

(c) The correct pitch and inflection are used. Some laugh lines depend on a drop or rise in inflection on the last word. The "throw-away" and "punch" come under this control. The *throw-away* is an immediate lowering in volume to a level that appears unprojected; the *punch* is led up to with clear pointing, pause, and then punching the key word.

(d) An effective facial expression is used.

(e) Business is precisely determined in relation to the line: whether it should come before or after delivery. Unless line and business serve one meaning, business executed as the line is delivered either destroys impact of the line or "kills" it.

(f) Finally, the proper rapport is established with the audience through exact timing in cue pickup, phrasing, and length of pause before the word or words that bring out the laugh.

These are major considerations that enter into comedy reading. How or to what extent they are used depends on the motivation for the comedy. In any event, the legitimate goal is to get the laugh. Once the laugh comes, however, another important control in timing must be considered.

3. Holding for a Laugh

There is good reason to hold for a laugh: If the actors continue their dialogue, either the laugh is cut short or the audience fails to hear the lines following the laugh. The solution is not simple: to have the actors hold or freeze for a laugh creates a static stage, which can prove dangerous to the vitality and pace of the scene, particularly if no laugh comes when expected. The experienced actor, adept at timing, keeps his stage alive by following through with gesture, business, or movement to fill the interval between start of laugh and attack on the next line. For the inexperienced, a director should initiate his cast to this technique during the latter stages of rehearsal. Some directors actually applaud at places where laughs are most likely to occur to give their cast a feeling of audience reaction. Previews accomplish the same more effectively.

The hold for a laugh is broken immediately after the laugh has reached its climax, not before. If the hold is extended, the pace slows down which, repeated each time a laugh occurs, dampens the momentum of the scene. However, when no laugh comes, the actor should not wait, otherwise the pause can be destructive to the pace. The dynamics of comic performance are at their best when laugh feeds on laugh. The experienced comic writers take this into account when structuring their scenes, but are at the mercy of the proficiency of actors and directors to make full use of the indications in the script, for these remain only indications until put to work in performance.

27

To keep up the pace, then, the laugh is never permitted to die out. The audience will still be on the down side of the laugh when the dialogue is picked up. The actor with the line pickup must punch the first words in order to arrest the audience's attention and bring the laughter, slowly subsiding, to a halt. There is psychological reasoning here, too. An audience that is not permitted to exhaust itself on any one laugh remains stimulated and eager to burst out on the next provocation—a valuable clue to generating and building up the audience's verve for laughter.

Mention must be made of uncontrolled laughter, which can be destructive to a performance. Usually it means that stimuli other than the character in the play are provoking laughter—a mishap, an awkward reaction, an amateurish reading. Legitimate or not, uncontrolled laughter is detrimental to the pace of the play if not brought firmly within control.

Casting and Rehearsals

Casting for Comedy

One of the challenging jobs that a director faces in the preliminaries of production is casting. Outside of precasting roles with known actors, casting is normally conducted by holding cold readings where the actor is handed the script on call; or by having the actor improvise on given circumstances; or through prepared auditions where the actor has studied and worked on the material beforehand. Beyond seeing that the external requirements for the character are met, the need is to check proficiencies in voice, speech, rhythm, and body control. Delivery, sense of timing, sustained energy, flexibility, and range of emotional expression must also be heard, seen, and felt. Prepared auditions, besides being more substantial, afford the director opportunity to use the actor's scene as a departure for further exploration of his potential for the role. The actor holds on to the characterization and lines he has prepared, and is asked to change only the given circumstance, attitude, locale, atmosphere, or tempo, singly or in combination as directed. In this approach, the actor, not hampered in searching for character traits or lines, is allowed more freedom to work on specifics and to reveal whatever his assets (or limitations) are.

Rehearsing Comedy

Freshness, spontaneity, and vitality are the sparks that incite the comic spirit, yet they are also the intangible qualities that can be lost in the laborious work-a-day rehearsals. Rehearsing comedy can be the most vacuous experience when scenes are played at a breathtaking pace in the early working periods. It becomes misspent energy, allowing no time for either investigation, reflection, experimentation, or the revelations that arise out of these. All are impossible to achieve in fast, runaway rehearsals that seem to fascinate some actors, even professionals. The cast is ready to rehearse for pace only after all aspects that make up a performance are firmly in hand. Pacing a scene or a play means that scenes are in control and, therefore, ready to be paced. Pace is timing, and timing implies that the material has been mastered. Approached in this manner, the miracle happens in the final days of rehearsal when, with the added excitement of pacing the show, freshness, spontaneity, and vitality blossom forth.

CHAPTER TWO

Farce

The primary intention of farce is to amuse by the invention of situations and incidents that embroil the characters in a way that excites laughter. To further provoke laughter, farce is "stuffed" with antics, ridiculous business, and gags—all directed at bringing enjoyment out of the physical characteristics of the situation.

A farce, furthermore, structures its story on a foundation of "possibility, but improbability." The events could happen, but probably never would. This improbability implies a release from conventional mode of behavior—a perpetration that tickles our fancy. The search for the lady's straw hat in Labiche's *An Italian Straw Hat*; the way the Sycamore family lives in Kaufman and Hart's *You Can't Take It With You*; the clerk's fling for adventure in Wilder's *The Matchmaker*; the sloppy habits of Oscar in Neil Simon's *The Odd Couple*—these characters flaunt their way of doing things against accepted patterns of social behavior and culture. The enjoyment comes out of the accumulation of incidents that involve the characters. The audience, never knowing what is coming up next, is kept in a continual state of excitement by surprise and shock as incidents catapult with accelerating speed through the progression of the story.

The openness of behavior, the direct statement of situation, the lack of penetration into the inner state of character, strip farce of any subtextual subtleties. All is externalized; all is to be taken at face value. This is particularly true of farces of situation.

TYPES OF FARCE

In line with the categories listed under comedy, farce also encompasses more than pure situation and tomfoolery. Farces like Priestley's *The Inspector General*, Kaufman and Hart's *You Can't Take It With You*, Giraudoux's *The Mad Woman of Chaillot*, and Durang's *Beyond Therapy* gain a great deal of their enjoyment through satire; others, more commonly accepted in the world of comedy, but basically framed in farce structure, like Coward's *Private Lives*, Wilde's *The Importance of Being Earnest*, and Stoppard's *Rosencrantz and Guildenstern Are Dead*, scintillate with witticisms; still others, like Shakespeare's *The Taming of the Shrew* and Moliere's *The Miser*, show more development in character than is necessary for the pure amusement of the situation. These are dimensions that go beyond the simple situation farces like Thomas' *Charley's Aunt* or Holm and Abbott's *Three Men on a Horse* and should be recognized in the interpretation and direction. However, to all intents they are farces in attitude, spirit, and sense of humor.

The world of farce is also inhabited by bitter grostesqueries of humor, as in Ionesco's *Rhinoceros*, Frisch's *Firebugs*, or John Guare's *The House of Blue Leaves*, where our most absurd thoughts are objectified or our most vile thoughts verbalized. Basically, the ridiculous antics come out of the same technique of immediacy of response without reflection. But unlike other farces, they are etched in the bitter bile of irony.

Farces, then, can also be enriched with ideas, satire, witticisms, skillfully drawn characters, and with eloquence in language and brilliancy of expression as we find in Shakespeare, Moliere, Anouilh, Wilde, and Stoppard. The great farce characters do achieve an individuality that has a poetic core and a potential for great suffering. We must not forget, however, that the primary purpose of farce is to amuse us.

DIRECTORIAL CONTROLS:
INTERPRETATION OF THE PLAY

The Essential Nature of Farce

The nature of farce is to *interest* us in the characters and situations, but not *involve* us in their problems. Since, in general, the main interest is situation, characters are by necessity rendered in bold simple strokes so that we can immediately grasp who and what they are. The easy recognition of character traits makes it possible to plunge them readily into complications once the groundwork is laid out. These are characters who react immediately by impulse and not through reflection and extended processes of thought. The two gentlemen in Moliere's *The Doctor in Spite of Himself* accept unequivocally the wife's statement that her woodman husband Sganarelle is a doctor, but will deny it unless he is beaten into admission. The husband is beaten and accepts the gentlemen's proposition to attend Geronte. And so it goes from action to action, not from a result of thinking, but from immediate emotional response. It is not a study of character per se, but a study of character in a predicament. We are not expected to sympathize or empathize with these highly etched characters so vibrantly alive with their own peculiarities. Be they cunning knaves, cheating husbands, shrewish housekeepers, we can laugh at their violent actions of bodily beatings, mishaps, and explosive confusions because we remain delighted observers of a world that gives release to our inhibitions and makes revelry and sport of our cherished etiquettes, modes, fashions, moralities, and institutions, without any resultant consequences to us.

Behaving as they do, the people of the farce world are not too discriminating. They never learn anything, never reason about what happens, never make rational inquiries. They are driven by a singleness of purpose. They remain abnormally insensitive to clues and are completely credulous about everything. Of course, if they behaved otherwise, the absurdities would never happen.

Understanding Why Farces Amuse Us

The major difference to comedy in what amuses an audience is that farce is free to release every restraint once the play is fully underway and the audience swept up in its exuberance. The ridiculous actions and antics are enjoyed vicariously: the dowager is kicked, the invective hurled, the lowliest insults the highest, dignities are annihilated.

Farce must be enjoyed in company. Laughter is contagious. Empty seats have an inhibiting effect on an audience's response. Professionals know that the fuller the house, the more responsive the audience; that a hearty laughter can be a great stimulant to generating outbursts of laughter from the entire audience. Bergson says it simply: "Laughter appears to stand in need of an echo."

Performance Values

A situation farce like *Charley's Aunt* presents the problem, as many farces do, of making the premise acceptable. This means that the performance cannot begin at too rapid a pace nor at an exaggerated scale. Pace and character actions must be at a level that communicates easily to an audience, in order to draw the audience into the play and have it become interested in characters and story. This is accomplished by detailing business for the characters, maintaining a subdued interplay of action between them, and keeping the overall picturization subtle. The lead into the premise, upon which the structure of the farce is built, must be carefully motivated, giving proper emphasis to the character reactions and lines which project the circumstances that brought about the particular activity. In *Charley's Aunt*, if Charley is to dress up in women's clothes, the action is made acceptable by his roommate proposing it in jest, followed by Charley's mock reiteration and final acceptance as the result of an emotional outburst. Business interpolations, lightness of touch, cue pickup, and character reactions that get laughs help in warming up the audience into the proper spirit.

The objective is to keep the audience from thinking of the improbability. Once the story is under way, the playing is enlarged, the tempo of scenes speeded, and movement and business introduced with little or no motivation and follow-through, although this last statement enters an area that can prove disastrous if either one is inappropiate to character and circumstances.

Dialogue in situation farce is sparsely written, colloquial to the circumstances, and uninvolved, permitting immediacy of reactions with rapid-fire give and take. It becomes stingy, racy, and violent as strong feelings and reactions mount and logic diminishes. The implication here is that humor does not depend on *what* is said, but on *how* it is said. The question of *how* is discussed later in this chapter under *business*.

DIRECTORIAL CONTROLS:
FUNDAMENTAL ELEMENTS OF DIRECTING

In general, the control of the fundamental elements of directing is based on comedic control. There are, however, certain considerations that apply particularly to farce.

Composition

The picture opens up to bring about a close rapport between character and audience and help create the proper climate for humor. For the same reason, scenes are played more in the downstage areas, except for overly violent actions where distance helps keep them in tone. Emphasis is direct. If it is the *how* of doing that gets the laugh, the attention of the audience had best be directed to where the *how* is taking place. Diversity of action can generate confusion and excitement when required by the situation, but carried out without purpose, selection, and control, it destroys meaning. Commotion and noise are rarely conducive to laughter.

Variety in areas, planes, levels, and body positions offers

other ways of stimulating and energizing scenes, besides the overused fast tempo.

Picturization

If characters in farce respond from emotion to emotion and are built out of a few telling traits, we should expect a clean line between action and reaction.

The continuous emotional responses to events happening in rapid succession are highly picturized and in this sense can be said to be exaggerated. Strong picturization indicates driving a moment to the hilt. Whatever the behavior, the actor performs with definition. Actions and reactions are spelled out: the audience is *told* and the audience *knows* by what it *sees* and *hears*, because the effort is there to *make* it *see* and *hear*. When, in *Three Men on a Horse*, the gamblers receive a phone call that the horse Irwin recommended is the winner, they pause, each facing the other, stunned by the news; they next turn in unison to stare at Irwin who sits alone with his drink, benignly unaware of what is happening. They fix their stare on him and *having established* the awesome admiration, move toward him. On reaching Irwin, there is a moment of hesitation before a burst of oversolicitous actions: one smoothes his hair, another dashes for an extra drink and hurries back, a third adjusts his chair and brushes his shoulder. The opportunities for business to express oversolicitude are as many as the circumstances and pacing of the scene allow.

Movement

Outside the normal use of movement, movements in farce can be choreographed along simple patterns. Repetition, imitation, sequence, and unison are some of the characteristic features. A movement toward an exit or an object is repeated several times; the swaying walk of one is imitated by another; several enter in sequence, from tall to taller to tallest and then to short—the entrance of shorty being the contrast and twist finish; several sit or rise in rhythmical succession; several sit and cross knees in unison. Parallel and countermovements are possible. Two characters pacing can move parallel with one another or in opposition, whereas if such patterns occurred in another type of play, they could register as forced or awkward. In farce, these typical movements, given proper motivation, are the visual stimulants to laughter.

Business

The derivative meaning of farce is "to stuff." Stuffing a line or an action can be considered an enrichment with business that derives from either the demands of the situation or the imaginative contributions of cast and director—contributions which should be appropiate to the characters and circumstances, and to their position in the play. However, in the delivery of lines devoid of humor, "stuffing" may become a necessity when a laugh is essential in maintaining the level of excitement.

"Gagging the line" becomes the technical tool.

Gags

A gag may be no more than a clearing of the throat, an imitation of a tone of voice, a shift of the eye, a flip of the handkerchief. Or they may be more extended intrusions: someone shouts and another works up to a louder shout, buts emits a hushed tone; or someone leaps over a chair and a second weakly simulates the action. The actions discussed under movement as typical to farce can also be called "gags." Gags, then, are interpolations of any kind that are not basically intrinsic or demanded by the circumstances, but are put in for their sheer value of getting laughs. Frequent use is made of them in farce, but a note of caution is in order: gags may be interpolations to those that work out the actions, but to the audience they must appear motivated. Charlie Chaplin offers this advice: "If a gag interfered with the logic of events, no matter how funny it was, I would not use it." Gags must seem to grow out of the situation.

DEMONSTRATION

The sweet young girl faints in the arms of a middle-age man, who tries to revive her. The man's wife, unbeknown to him, appears at the window watching. In the attempt to hold up the girl, he gets entangled in arms and legs. Both fall to the ground with the girl on top. The wife is aghast. He tries to maneuver her up but again loses balance, this time landing on top of her (consternation from the wife). The action can be stretched according to the ingenuity of the participants and the feeling of how much and how far to "gag" the moment within the circumstances and dynamics of the scene.

Atmosphere and Mood

The same considerations apply to farce as those discussed in the chapter on comedy.

Rhythm

The basic rhythm of farce is light and bouncy, and moves trippingly along. It does not rush headlong at a furious tempo. Nor does it run roughshod over any attempt to point and delineate lines and reactions, to sharpen contrasts, to use variations in tempo, to build up incongruities, to relish business and unexpected turn of events, to delight in zany mannerisms, etc. Yet none of these, even though cleanly executed, provoke laughter unless they are properly timed. Unfortunately, proper timing and delineation can be lost in the tendency to have farce played at a rapid tempo. Ultimately, it depends on controlling the pace of the performance.

Maintaining the pace comes out of the forward movement, the anticipation, which is instilled in the audience by the control of a cumulative effect discussed below and by the constant indications that an action or a remark is leading to something. Pace comes out of keeping the audience deliciously stimulated by surprises, and tantalized in anticipation of what is to follow.

OTHER CONSIDERATIONS IN DIRECTING FARCE

Plotting on a Cumulative Scale

The control of movement and business must always be related to what has preceded and to what is to follow. It comes from somewhere, it goes to something ahead. This sense of progression affects not only proportioning, but also phrasing in a sequence of actions. An action that is complete in itself may be beautifully executed, but it creates a static performance. Movement and business should be plotted on a cumulative scale.

DEMONSTRATION

The duel scene in Twelfth Night (act III, scene iv)
The duel between Aguecheek and Viola (disguised as Sebastian) starts off—after a sequence of cajoling, encouragements, and threats by Sir Toby and Fabian—with Aguecheek and Viola each afraid to approach the other. They are vigorously spurred on by Sir Toby and Fabian.

(1) They touch swords and scamper back. More frights, more encouragements, more refusals, until Sir Toby and Fabian each take hold of the "combatants'" fencing arms and practically fence for them.

(2) Aguecheek and Viola pull away, leaving the two duelling unaware of the fact for a few beats.

(3) Aguecheek and Viola, taking advantage, tiptoe off in opposite directions, but are caught and hurriedly brought back to positions.

(4) More protestations until in the struggle Viola, egged on by Fabian, unintentionally thrusts her sword forward. Aguecheeck collapses from fright on seeing the blade in front of him.

(5) Viola, thinking she has drawn blood turns away and collapses against Fabian. Aguecheek revives, sees her fright, and this time courageously attacks wildly.

(6) Viola, in consternation, suddenly turns on him,

whacking him with such abruptness that he screams and runs—straight into the arms of Antonio, who whips out his sword to second Viola (Sebastian to him).

(7) Aguecheek, seeing the outhrust sword of Antonio, collapses gracefully.

This accumulation of actions is structured to climax in the confrontation with Antonio which, in turn, prepares for the brief but exciting duel between Antonio and Sir Toby.

The technique of accumulation has a special application in the repetition of any movement or business designed to get a laugh. It takes the first and the second moves to establish the pattern, and the third, with the unexpected twist, to get the laugh. Three repetitions, but with the third having the surprise ending.

Acting in Farce

For the actor, the challenge in performing farce is to create a person who, while in the throes of the circumstances and predicaments, still appears to have a probable living identity rather than a caricature exhibiting overblown comic traits. Characters and their actions may strike the audience as ridiculous and ludicrous, but not so for the actor. Farce characters never realize they are funny. The few comic characteristics that make up the character must be completely justified by the actor. The actor, as in most types of plays, must play *in* and not *at* the character. We play *at* character by burlesquing, parodying him, or acting the role as a travesty. These are legitimate types in themselves, but not farce. Unfortunately, farce is often mistakenly performed somewhere near the borderline of these perfectly acceptable treatments of criticism and ridicule.

The problem of acting farce can be clarified if the actor keeps in mind the singleness of purpose that drives the farcical character to action. To achieve this singleness of purpose, the character must be stripped down to a singular trait: the *bullheaded* detective determined to hunt down his man and the *naive* clerk anxious to return to his job. If obstacles interfere, and the bull-headed detective believes the naive clerk to be his man, and each drives hard toward his objective, we have a situation that can explode in number of directions.

If we appreciate the inner drive that moves the farce character with urgent dynamic intent, we can understand the true meaning of the statement that farce playing is broad and exaggerated. Otherwise, these words taken at face value can lead to acting that is external and empty in gesture. This strong inner drive, this strict determination to reach the objective, does not permit involved processes of thought. Though there is sincerity in feeling and communication, the immediacy of response leads to feelings that ride the crest—which is what essentially happens to make farce work.

Acting in farce calls for effortless flexibility in voice and body: a mobile face, an ability for mimicry through voice and gesture, a gracefulness in mime. It is a flexibility, however, that is limited by the external requirements made on character, and which, in turn, accounts for some of the reasons for type casting.

Casting and Rehearsals

Casting for Farce

A good start for humor in farce can be made with the external appearance of characters. For this reason we may be interested, depending on the nature of the farce, in assembling a cast that includes contrasting types, physically and vocally: the tall with the short, the lean with the fat, the awkward lanky with the prim plump; or in the vocal range, the nasal with the tremulous, the high-pitched with the drawl. Farce delights in incongruities: the strong, robust laborer with a peep of a voice, the imposing chairman of the board who breaks down and cries, the full-bodied, rugged mover carrying the vase while his insignificant bit of an assistant struggles along with an overstuffed chair, or the sweet youngster with a deep baritone.

These visual and auditory aspects of characterizations become an important contribution to the humor, provided care is taken that they are not deformities. Playing deformities can offend and alienate an audience, but the unique voice, manner, or physique, accentuated by the proper costume, can create a comic picture when introduced under the right circumstances. Comedians have built their reputation on their unique peculiarities. Jimmy Durante's nose and gravel voice served as his comic "mask," as did Paul Lynde's tremulous voice and facial contortions. A study of the popular comedian's "mask" and individual manner of vocal and physical control is valuable for a fuller awareness of comic characterization.

Rehearsing Farce

Laughter is an integral part of the play's dynamics. The truth of this is seen in the latter days of rehearsals when the actors, fully versed in the play, try their best to throw off a growing feeling of insecurity from the emptiness that greets their rehearsal performance. All seems ridiculous and absurd, and rightly so since the conditions are artificial. It is not an exaggeration to say that under the conditions of rehearsal, farce is non-existent, for its life-giving forces are the responses from the audience.

This awareness that farce comes into its own when performed before an audience is an important insight for the director, since it is a guide to his control of rehearsals. To achieve the absolute clarity in delineation demanded by farce, everything should be worked out carefully and meticulously during the early stages of rehearsals. Appropriateness, selection, and proportioning continually come into play for each bit of business, gesture, line delivery, and so on. When to do, what to do, and how often to do it are crucial matters that have to be determined. Line readings and their handling should be tested until the most effective ones are found. The overall situation should be fully laid out. A situation farce, for example, should be sketched in early so that circumstances, points of entrance, and areas of playing are established, thus setting the groundwork for rehearsing the meat of the farce—the *how* of actions, the gags or interpolations, the tempo accelerations in their cumulative sequences. The actual pacing—a major contribution to the ultimate vitality of farce—is left until the final stages of rehearsals. When actors know what to do, and have this knowledge deeply engrained, they then can begin to play the scene for its dynamics, generating new discoveries, and in so doing, spontaneity—quite different from the doldrums felt by a cast when a farce is rehearsed at a fast pace, never permitting detailed analysis, study, exploration, or experimentation.

CHAPTER THREE

Tragedy

Tragedy in its simpliest terms contains three basic distinguishing elements: (1) an uncontrollable destroying force; (2) the one who is destroyed or the victim; and (3) the will or desire of the victim to fight against the force and not be destroyed. If the victim or *protagonist* is unsuccessful in his fight against the force of the *antagonist*, the play, with its action completed, ends as a tragedy. However, the destruction of the protagonist does not necessarily mean his death. Nor does the story of the protagonist struggling in vain constitute a tragedy. The true tragedy has an additional factor that creates an emotional state of pity—an emotional contact between play and audience that at the end of the play leaves the audience with a feeling of exaltation rather than depression. This inner release or moral purging of the emotions is called a *catharsis*.

Before elaborating on the personal yet universal response of catharsis, more facts about the basic elements should be recognized: the destruction of the protagonist, whether within or outside the character, is inevitable rather than by chance or caprice; the protagonist, in defiance, ultimately gains perception in the moment of catastrophe—his spirit triumphs, bringing his tragedy to an affirmative resolution. It is this perception and affirmation on the part of the protagonist that is the catalyst to the catharsis experienced by the audience, which implies that tragedy deals with struggles that we understand and ap-

43

preciate. Actions cannot be too extravagant nor too removed from ordinary life. They are struggles of universal significance that throw light upon the human condition. The audience is able to experience the emotional state of the protagonist, participate in his revelation, and pity him in his struggle. Tragedy happens to people, placing its faith in the value and dignity of the individual. It reassures belief in man's destiny and the ultimate triumph of good. It affirms man's capacity for greatness.

TYPES OF TRAGEDY

Taking a less limiting definition of tragedy, the control of dramatic values can be extended to cover a wide range of plays that deal with the serious aspects of life. These are plays such as social and domestic dramas, where idea, character, and story connote a larger reference than the events of any one individual.

DIRECTORIAL CONTROLS: INTERPRETATION OF THE PLAY

The Essential Nature of Tragedy

Philosophers express the view that though there is social and scientific progress in society, there is no moral progress in the birth-death cycle of the individual. In the accumulated experience of mankind, the human psyche remains the same. Emotions, passions, and drives are discovered anew each generation and through each individual. Herein lies the tragedy of being human. But while man's nature, desire, and drives may remain the same, his problem with nature, society, and himself has over the ages been explored and expressed in various ways and with varying shifts of emphasis in depicting the "uncontrollable destroying force."

Historically, the drama of the early Greeks presented the protagonist in conflict with fate: Agamemnon dies because of the curse on the House of Atreus; Oedipus is condemned because the ironic hand of destiny leads him to murder his father and live incestuously with his mother—tragic irony, where the audience knows the protagonist's fate, which he in time discovers. The Elizabethan drama, in probing the inner world of the character, presents the protagonist in conflict with human failings such as jealousy, pride, and false ambition that become the "tragic flaw." French Renaissance and English Restoration drama has the protagonist in conflict between the social code of honor and love's passion, as in Racine's *Phaedre* and Congreve's *Love for Love*. Nineteenth century drama pits man, the protagonist, against justice, conventional behavior, and heredity, as in the plays of Bruckner, Sardou, and Ibsen. Twentieth century drama expands the pattern of the individual's refusal to succumb to conformity, and adds the urges of the subconscious, and the inability of man to communicate with man through plays like those of Ionesco, Pinter, and Albee. But for these latter writers and others of the contemporary scene, tragedy in the traditional sense is nonexistent in a world where man holds the power to immediate and universal self-destruction.

DIRECTORIAL CONTROLS:
FUNDAMENTAL ELEMENTS OF DIRECTING

A major consideration in directing tragedy and serious drama is to project the elements at conflict: the nature of the uncontrollable force must be made clear and the actions depicting the protagonist's will to fight this force must be pointedly emphasized. We must know *who* is in conflict with *what*, and the *purpose* that drives the protagonist to *be* in conflict. The reasons that motivate the protagonist to action must be carefully projected in order for the audience to understand and empathize with these drives. Several controls through the use of the fundamentals of directing are at our disposal to achieve these objectives.

Composition

Out of the many lines of dialogue in the play, the audience's attention should be centered on the pertinent lines noted in the initial phase of script preparation that relate to the elements in conflict and to the various forces and character drives. Emphasis through composition offers one of the means in accomplishing this. Along with bringing emphasis to the speaking character, a proper reading of the significant dialogue lifts it out of the body of the speech. The kind of movement, whether positive or negative, the use made of business, and the tempo of the moment, are additional controls in line emphasis.

Picturization

Actions that show the progressive downfall of the protagonist as he struggles against the opposing force are fully picturized, so that, as in a film strip, the main struggle could be depicted through the selection of key scenes. To fully picturize means that these scenes are given dramatic extension by stretching out a reaction, deepening a moment of realization, sharpening a contrast, and bringing focus to the character. The demonstration from *The Cherry Orchard*, in chapter one, on playing serious scenes in comedy elaborates on this control. Though it remains within the director's control to give added weight to any one scenic moment, whatever is done must be appropiate to the characters and circumstances of the scene, and continually evaluated in reference to the entire play.

The same control of picturizing actions to give them dramatic significance holds true for scenes that contain the *justifications* behind a character's behavior or that show the character in some state of inner conflict, in light of the brutal deeds he is about to commit or has committed. If we are to gain the audience's pity or sympathy for protagonists like Macbeth or Othello, the scenes that project a deeper understanding of their actions or of the forces at work on them must also be given significance.

46

Movement

The connotative values of composition and movement can also be used effectively to accentuate the dramatic significance of a specific situation and make it easier for an audience to feel and sense more acutely a particular scene as it relates to story, character, or theme. This is a control of a sequence of movements into a unified design—a *pattern of movement* created to emphasize the interplay of character on character.

DEMONSTRATION

Othello, *act III, scene iii. [Desdemona and Emilia have just exited, leaving Othello alone with Iago.]*

OTHELLO *[looking after Desdemona]* Perdition catch my soul but I do love thee!

From this affirmation of love to the confrontation between Othello and Iago (Othello: "By heaven, I'll know thy thoughts.") to Iago's exit and Othello's self-inflicting quandary immediately followed by Desdemona's re-entrance (Othello: "Look! where she comes. If she be false, O! then heaven mocks itself."), Shakespeare dramatizes a sequence of interplay of character on character which for greatest effectiveness can be conceived in patterns of movement that tell the story choreographically. Iago plays his game with subtle advances and retreats, each time drawing Othello to him as he plants the seed of Desdemona's "adultery" in Othello's mind.

The struggle showing Iago gaining his objective, then losing ground, then attacked and attacking (the confrontation), can be rendered in a pattern of movement that describes the ups and downs of the struggle in visual terms, without dialogue.

Projecting the basic situation in graphic terms gives the director the general blocking for a scene that is conceived out of textual demands. Instead of treating movement in isolated instances, purpose and direction is brought to the staging, making the movements an integral part of a design that accentuates the dramatic intent of the entire scene.

Business

Because serious drama depends on a strong tie between play and audience for its emotional impact, important factors in control that help strengthen this hold are simplicity and directness. This implies that only the essentials of business are selected in order not to blur actions with details, especially in scenes of direct conflict between characters, where business details should be at a minimum or completely eliminated. Pantomime is not elaborate. Attention is maintained on the dramatic significance of character and dialogue, and any enrichment with business should be used only as a further means of delineating the text, and not to attract attention to itself.

Atmosphere, Mood, and Rhythm

For an analysis of atmosphere, mood, and rhythm, and the interaction of one on the other, see the following sections on *Intensification and the Tragic Tone* and *Economy of Means*.

OTHER CONSIDERATIONS IN DIRECTING TRAGEDY

Intensification and the Tragic Tone

The controls discussed under composition, picturization, movement, and business are the means of clarifying for an audience the elements of drama in conflict. Actually, these are controls through which we *intensify* a specific moment for greater impact. Intensification is a positive and vital attribute of the dramatic, quite in contrast to the "tragic tone" or "tragic rhythm" often assumed when acting or directing a serious drama or tragedy. Tragedies do not demand slow, ponderous playing, with voices that intone the doom. Tragedy is vital and dynamic—the gamut of emotions is its life blood. Granted that the playwright takes a serious attitude toward his subject matter, it is the outcome that makes the tragedy. The playwright begins his story at a point out of which tragedy develops. Translated into directorial terms, this means that the control of *rhythm* and *mood* is kept in balance with the writer's intentions and structuring. In *Othello*, the relationship between Othello and his wife Desdemona, regardless of parental disapproval and the concern of war, is one where both are completely immersed in love and respect for each other. They are in ecstasy over the joyous wonder of it all. The culminating point occurs in act III, scene iii, referred to earlier, when Othello calls out after her: "Excellent wretch! Perdition catch my soul but I do love thee! and when I love thee not, chaos is come again." Shakespeare, the craftsman, immediately juxtaposes Iago's "My noble lord . . . Did Michael Cassio, when you wooed my lady, know of your love . . . ?" And thus the demoniacal scheme leading to Othello's destruction is put into action by Iago. Before this, stress should be given to those moments where Desdemona and Othello declare their love for one another. We want their marriage to succeed against the opposition of prejudice and treachery. Intensification through rhythmic contrasts, rather than heavy drenching, is the keynote to strong dynamics. The task in directing tragedy is to clarify the elements at conflict and to project these dynamically. An audience's positive response arises out of this kind of understanding and control, and not out of soaking the play in continuous solemn moods.

Economy of Means

Economy of means is a mark of distinction in all art. Though its application varies according to the requirements of the specific work, in general it implies that *nothing else is done except that which contributes to the desired impression or expression.*

Whenever possible, one action should signify more than one dimension. Implicit in *economy of means* is the idea that the most possible must be achieved with each stroke of direction. If picturization and movement of a scenic moment strengthen its emotional content and reinforce the empathic response between it and the audience, then they become effective visual controls the director can use in projecting the seriousness of the moment without resorting to mournful tones or wringing the moment through creeping actions. If the scenic moment is further strengthened by the connotative values of composition and movement, then *mood* is added to the visual interpretation with a single stroke of direction. Through controls as these, the peaceful and relaxed atmosphere of one scene can be contrasted to the disturbed and restless elements of another. The mood and atmosphere of the first scene is achieved through the use of horizontal lines, curved form, and closed-in groupings; the contrasting scene, through irregularity in form and diffused mass created primarily by variety in level and body positions as the characters move to different areas on their reactions. A reaction may be the turn of the body in the chair; or intensified by having the character rise; or further intensified by having the character move away after rising. The physical extension given a reaction and the direction of movement, whether up- or downstage, or onto a level, are dependent on the mood demands of the text. With this potential of intensifying mood through the connotative use of composition and movement, flexibility in control is at the director's disposal to achieve more than one dimension with each action of blocking.

Ground Plan and Fundamental Design

The thematic values of a play can stimulate a design for the ground plan which incorporates the forces at work and which in turn sets the basic movements of the scene: entrances, exits, positions for sitting, area use, and other movements motivated by the situation. In arriving at the fundamental design, the meaning of the act is determined and then interpreted in terms of areas, levels, lines, emphasis, and so on, so that the composition of the ground plan and staging of the action are expressive of the idea. Together they give the design for the main action of an act or for the entire play. It is an approach based on the concept of pattern of movement described in the section on movement.

DEMONSTRATION

Chekhov's The Cherry Orchard, *act II*. [*The open country. Sunset. Summer.*]

[*Lyubov, her family and retainers, Trofimov, and Lopakhin are gathered in the garden by the tumbledown shrine. Lyubov and daughters are seated on the old garden bench.*]

The placement of the bench at center stage within the confinements of a low, crumbled wall can be derived out of the thematic statement of the play—that societies centered in a world of their own, where vital ties with the outer world are severed and responsibilities no longer respected, will be pushed aside by the very people once dependent on them for a livelihood. The positioning of the characters (seated at the bench, standing outside the wall, lost in the shadows of a crumbling shrine), the picturization of a huddled group, the direction of entrances, the movement from area to area—these are specifics of actions within a ground plan conceived out of a fundamental design.

Story and character needs have called for certain reactions which are channeled into movements, but with design in mind there is no pondering "where do they move now?" Fundamental or thematic design sets the basis of the direction and area of character movements.

Playing Comedy Scenes in Serious Plays

In serious plays the comic scenes afford relief from the predominant mood, but they are not performed for a heightened comic effect as they are in comedy. Classic examples are the scenes of the porter in *Macbeth* and the gravediggers in *Hamlet*. As "relief scenes," these bring a breath of refreshment to the audience after a highly emotionally charged sequence of scenes—a kind of rest period from the sustained emotional involvement.

Played without boundaries of restraint, these comic relief scenes could shatter the threshold of belief that must be maintained. The audience, emotionally involved in the play, cannot be expected to respond openly to a scene that calls for laughter; and neither can they be expected to be immediately immersed in an emotional scene that follows moments of hilarity. These sharp contrasts require time for adjustment. The practised playwright accounts for this with careful preparation and motivations, as witness the transition made for the porter in *Macbeth* by the knocks at the gate, and that for the gravediggers in *Hamlet* by the opening informative dialogue. Plays that lack these transitions in writing need the same meticulous attention for the audience's emotional adjustment. Refer to chapter one, *Playing Serious Scenes in Comedy*, for elaboration on this point.

Casting and Rehearsals

Casting Serious Plays
The physical and vocal qualities of the actor unmistakably contribute to the final impression made by a scene. Beyond the requirements called for by the text for specific characters, an actor's total physical and vocal needs are considered in relation to the type of play. Whereas in farce wide contrasts in voice and physique can be enriching assets, in tragedy the tonal qualities of voice and physical proportions between characters should bear less contrasts to one another. Strong contrasts introduce disproportion, which is a needless factor unless re-

quired and contributive to the values of the play. Normally, voices should be vibrant, warm and colorful in texture, flexible in range and melody, and strong in sustaining power.

Rehearsing Serious Plays

In plays where the major interest is in character, it is helpful to the actor to rehearse his scenes in sequence. This is especially advantageous in Shakespearean plays, where scenes for any one character are dispersed. Rehearsing the actor's specific scenes in a unified sequence brings the role boldly into comparison with the rest of the play. The advantages are many: the actor becomes more alert to the pertinent steps in the progression of character revelation and to the controls he must exercise in selection and emotional balance. The changes in relationship between his role and other characters become more distinct; and his sensitivity to the acceleration and build toward crises and climax more acute.

CHAPTER FOUR

Melodrama

Melodrama can be as emotionally serious as tragedy, but with the underlying optimism and happy ending of comedy. Its primary purpose is to excite and thrill the audience vicariously, through scenes of suspense and strong tensions. Its serious mood is often broken with contrasting scenes of amusement from the comedy characters, as in the unexpected appearance of the detective in *Dial M for Murder*. Structurally, it places its major interest on plot, on "how is it all going to turn out?"

G. B. Shaw defines melodrama in these terms: "Melodrama is made up of simple and sincere actions and feelings appealing to the mass audience in its straightforward philosophy, passion, and motives, and relieved by plenty of fun; and for variety, using broad contrasts between types."

TYPES OF MELODRAMA

Each type of melodrama makes its appeal so pointedly out of a special interest that the several types fall readily into popular categories. The value of classifying and appreciating the special interest rests again on the necessity of furnishing ourselves with a source of reference for analysis and interpretation as aids toward directorial controls.

Situation Melodramas

The writers of thrillers of action and intrigues for stage, film, and television set the standard for situation melodramas. Originally, melodramas were plays in which music was employed to underscore the dramatic episodes or substitute for dialogue—soft, soothing music for beautiful thoughts; agitated and tumultuous music for thoughts of violence and revenge.

This kind of programmatic music was used prolifically in the early vintage of sentimental and action films which transposed to the screen the popular theatricalities of the late nineteenth century stage: unadulterated, simply rendered characters (pure hero, virtuous heroine, unrepenting villain, unquestioning and understanding companion), heightened tensions, strong interplay of emotions seasoned with sentiment, extended scenes of suspense, climactic progression from one physical action to another, sharp contrasts from scenes of violence to tender love scenes or comedy scenes bordering on farce. Though these works romanticized life, they did so through an actuality with which the audience identified. There is exciting realism to such actions as fist and gun fights, fires, escapades, accidents, collisions. The appeal of action dramas continue to rely on the same qualities of actuality and common behavior, even though the events may be outside our daily experience. These are qualities that draw an audience into the life of this contrived world, beyond the thrills they receive from the other elements.

Mystery and Murder Melodramas

In this category of situation melodramas can also be placed the mystery, murder, ghost, and horror plays, many of which fall into the class of "who-done-its," in which the audience is kept on edge by the mystery of the culprit's identity, as in Agatha Christie's plays. The expectancy of how the murderer will be found out in Knott's *Dial M for Murder* and Priestley's *An In-*

spector Calls, the unexpected reversals of victim and perpertrator baffling and shocking the audience with their sadistic battle of wits and role-playing in Shaffer's *Sleuth* and Levin's *Death Trap*, fascinate by the clever manipulation of plot.

Psychological Melodramas

In psychological melodramas, the development of action grows out of the psychosis of the main driving character, as in Patrick Hamilton's *Angel Street*, Percy and Denham's *Ladies in Retirement*, Emlyn William's *Night Must Fall*, and similar plays where the characters are portrayed in a seemingly deeper dimension. In these the behavior of the psychotic becomes an intriguing case study. Actually, it is not the playwright's intention to penetrate into character to the ultimate of self-revelation and evaluation. Rather, his method is to reveal the psychosis early in the story and to use it as the catalyst that sets up the situation, thereby creating tensions and suspense to a tautness eventually relieved by the capture, suicide, killing, or whatever, of the character harboring the psychosis.

Melodramas of Ideas

Adding dimension to character are melodramas of ideas in which a philosophic concept underscores the situation, and in which characters intellectualize their motives. In Sherwood's *Petrified Forest*, Pirandello's *Henry IV*, Sartre's *No Exit*, Peter Weiss' *Marat/Sade*, and Camus' *Caligula*, ideas are the guiding elements of the plays.

Each play demonstrates its central theme by involving characters in situations and circumstances expressive of that idea. In *Petrified Forest*, Sherwood believes that the man of culture is petrified in his own intellectual sphere, and that the brute forces of humanity will take over the world. In demonstrating this, he creates circumstances of an intellectual pitted against a hunted gangster. Disregarding Sherwood's symbolism in character and actions in this realistic melodrama, the play generates its suspense and excitement out of pure situation, and ultimately even the good triumphs.

Sartre's *No Exit* has man trapped in his conscience and sets up circumstances to dramatize that hell is the everyday existence of living with our fellow beings. He localizes the action in a tastefully designed living room which, however, is in limbo on the borders of hell. The attempt and inability to escape, the horror of what lies beyond the exit, the suspicions and tensions among the three characters, enmesh them in a taut melodrama enriched by tantalizing teasers from the intellectual sparring.

Camus' *Caligula* is a devastating horror story rooted in idea. The causes of violence are not seated in any psychosis or emotional upset of the main character, but grow out of careful analytic reasoning that lays bare the illogicality and hypocrisy of man's behavior to man.

DIRECTORIAL CONTROLS:
INTERPRETATION OF THE PLAY

The Essential Nature of Melodrama

In melodrama, there is no need for the playwright to penetrate deeply into the psychological and sociological background of character per se, since his interest is not to present a character study, but rather to involve his characters—rendered sufficiently to satisfy the demands of plot—into predicaments through which he can create tensions and build suspense. What they say and do is not for the purpose of revealing depths of character or great truths, but to advance the story's plot complications in order to generate heightened excitement and sensation. The hero is noble by innate trait of character rather than through any growth in understanding the reasons for his actions. Even in psychological melodramas, where interest in character is strong, the characters are primarily created to perform the tasks assigned. Character motivations and subtleties are subordinated to the drive for action, suspense, and surprise.

Life is narrowed to its most telling actions, with no unnecessary details. This interest on plot and subsequent emphasis on situation can also be seen through the frequent use of wordless scenes to advance the action of the play.

Understanding Why Melodramas Intrigue Us

The popular intrigue and adventure stories in television and motion pictures are excellent examples of thoroughbred melodramas of their type. They grip and wring the audience's emotions with plots of near catastrophes, hair-raising encounters, exaltation of virtue and poetic justice—each satisfying the audience's desire to see its "romantic imaginings" acted out. The underlying optimism of melodrama, furthermore, prevents the audience from sinking into despair, since it knows that in the end the suffering heroes will overcome all obstacles through their alertness, physical strength, or sheer good luck.

This popularity also stems from the feeling of actuality that melodrama projects. Its hold on an audience depends on this sense of recognition and identification with character and circumstance. This is furthered by the treatment of dialogue that has an everyday feeling about it and is written without pretenses at high literary qualities. Because of this easy identification, the normally unusual situations and unique circumstances become acceptable, as do the characters' insensitivity or oversensitivity to plot clues.

The continuing appeal of Shakespeare's tragedies is in part to be credited to the melodramatic structure of these plays. Strip the text of character probings and profundities, of philosophic and moral perceptions, and there remains an excitingly moving story plotted with complications of incidents, unusual circumstances, and contrasting scenes of amusement from the comedy characters, designed to electrify and thrill the audience. There is truth in the statement that "melodrama is the skeleton of enduring tragedy."

Performance Values and Controls

The director must recognize the playwright's intention and emphasis in his analysis of a melodrama, for it is through controls in interpretation, acting, and other directorial means that these plays are enriched. Proper emphasis is placed on those elements of the play that need extra support because of overbalance in character psychosis, discussion, or situation.

In psychological or thematic melodramas, for example, where the playwright's intent goes beyond that of presenting a suspenseful entertainment, it is logical to build up the situation. In these plays the control is a reversal of what is usually meant by "bringing out the subtext." Here the major emphasis is so strongly on psychological probings or discussion, social or otherwise, that it becomes important to maintain suspense by playing up the underlying circumstances or predicament through picturization. Creation of movement and business arises from an understanding of the implied circumstances surrounding the characters who are involved in intellectual or psychoanalytic pursuits. The scene as written is dominated by direct expression of issues. Unless the director realizes that underneath the talk there is tension and conflict, the suspense that should keep the audience on edge will be diluted and the talk will become rhetoric, shorn of dramatic interest.

In melodramas where situation is foremost but the full value of the script dependent on thematic implication, idea lines should be stressed and characters enriched. Deficiencies in the script, whether through weak writing or gaps in dialogue, are improved by the way a line is read. A scene that otherwise might sound trite and thin is given significance by adding weight to a reading through reflection, tone of voice, and proper gesture to accompany the delivery. This kind of mental penetration, when produced deliberately and executed carefully, brings out traits of character where none actually exist. It is in the nature of situation melodrama, with its emphasis on intrigue and suspense, to minimize character richness. The writer resorts to types whose habits and idiosyncrasies are readily comprehended, so that he can move on with the story. For many reasons, then, it is necessary to strengthen character or situation. Some of the considerations for control follow.

To strengthen character:

1. Seek out the moral conflicts and play these moments fully.

2. Bring complete process of thought to the readings of lines. Have the actor deliberate.

3. Bring detail to the manners and traits of character.

To strengthen situation:

1. Bring out and heighten story and suspense values of the pertinent dialogue and actions.

2. Have the actor play the situation without overreacting subjectively to events.

3. Bring focus to the event in action.

4. Heighten the emotional significance of a moment by building up the details through picturization.

5. Increase the amount of movement to heighten action. Care must be taken, however, to subordinate movement to the inner rhythm of character.

6. Have the actor execute his pantomime meticulously and deliberately to give actuality to the situation and to draw every possible effect out of it. As the intensity of a scene builds, the details of picturization and business are minimized.

7. Play with great contrasts and variations in tempo implied by the given circumstances.

DIRECTORIAL CONTROLS:
FUNDAMENTAL ELEMENTS OF DIRECTING

In the case of melodrama, a clearer understanding of the controls of the fundamentals can be achieved through a study of their interrelation in the following discussion of special characteristics.

DIRECTORIAL CONTROLS: SPECIAL CHARACTERISTICS
Suspense Scenes and Teasers

Probably the outstanding characteristic of melodrama is the build in suspense gained through plotting and the enrichment of actions by the use of *teasers*. The teaser is any kind of delaying action that heightens the suspense of the outcome by its intrusion in building toward a climax.

DEMONSTRATION

Two men are leisurely drinking wine and discussing some social or philosophic subject. Here the audience's interest is focused on the ideas under discussion.

Now, introduce a teaser: one of the glasses of wine is poisoned. The situation shifts to suspense, with the audience wondering, "How is it going to turn out?"

The scene has taken on melodramatic qualities. This effectiveness in building up suspense scenes to greater suspense and anticipation justifies their use.

DEMONSTRATION

A soldier is being hunted by his foe in enemy territory and is befriended by a farmer who hides him in the loft of his humble home.

Teaser #1. The farmer, having bolted his door, realizes that the ladder leading to the loft is in sight. At this moment the foe knocks.

The delaying action brought about by the need to remove the ladder before opening the door heightens the suspense of the scene. This action, if not in the text, could be created by the director; so could all teasers below, if the intent of the scene were primarily to thrill the audience. When and when not to use teasers is dependent on the overall dramatic value of the play. If the purpose of creating the hunt was for thematic reasons—to bring out the moral values of a soldier in confrontation with an enemy farmer who befriends him—then the foe's knock and questioning of the farmer could be enacted in a direct manner and done away with immediately, bringing the focus fully on the thematic implications. However, continuing with the delaying action of teasers or "stretching the elastic" to heighten suspense:

Teaser #2. The foe enters, removes his hat, and sits during the questioning to catch his breath. The sitting is a secondary objective to tantalize the audience.

Teaser #3. Blood drips from the loft to a conspicuous spot on the floor, but during the questioning the farmer stands between it and the foe.

Teaser #4. The foe, satisfied that the farmer has not seen the soldier, leaves. He is out the door and the farmer about to close the door, when the foe re-enters. He has forgotten his hat.

Teaser #5. On his way out, the foe slips on the wet spot on the floor caused by the dripping blood. The scene holds for a moment of concern. The farmer breaks the tension by immediately coming to his rescue, while the foe laughs over his clumsiness. The foe exits.

The continual occurrence of suspense scenes with or without teasers keeps the audience in a state of tension. We should make the most of them, but without laboring the issue.

Other Contributary Factors in Building Suspense

Besides "stretching the elastic" with teasers, tension is also increased by building up atmospheric details. Effects and offstage noises like creaking doors, footsteps, ticking clocks, thunder, rain, lightning, and so forth are an integral part of the melodramatic vocabulary. Details in setting and properties also reinforce the mood of these scenes: heavy tapestries and furniture, cobwebs, hunter's trophies, and items of menace warrant careful selection in keeping with the overall tonality of the play. Music, either contrasting or in harmony with the mood depending on what is most effective, has a long heritage in its contribution to melodrama. The tendency in the contemporary theatre is to motivate the source of music through hi-fis, radio, and so on.

Tempo Changes and "Shockers"

Techniques of building to a climax with a sudden drop scene are "shockers" that give melodrama its edge. This is one aspect of tempo control, which is an important tool in creating the required tensions.

DEMONSTRATION

A party of fun and games is punctuated with growing hilarity. Suddenly, a bloodcurdling scream offstage pierces the scene. Silence, followed by a long pause. Then, whispering behind the door; all focus on door as it opens slowly (the door opens onstage, hinged downstage so as to block the view from the audience). All step back, aghast! Lights fade out and curtain!

Another control is executing a bit of business or movement with deliberateness. A slow tempo, with deliberate detailing, is a technique that holds the attention of the audience. An example is the action in Joseph Kesselring's melodramatic farce *Arsenic and Old Lace* when Jonathan, the maniacal nephew, ties up his victim and meticulously arranges the surgical instruments to "operate" on him. The deliberateness works like a charmer, "mesmerizing" the audience through its strong attractive pull.

Relief Scenes

Release from the sustained suspense and moody atmospheres, which if overextended can wear down an audience, comes from the love and comedy scenes in the play. These are the *relief scenes* that allow the director opportunity to break the tensions built up in the audience. The contrasts offered by these scenes to the basic mood bring added vitality and excitement provided they are performed within the momentum reached at that point. More than not, some kind of urgency, which is a tempo factor, colors the circumstances. Actually, relief scenes whet an audience's appetite for the ensuing scenes of high tension.

The Plant

The plant is a subtle insertion of dialogue, business, or action, the significance of which escapes the audience until its final use is revealed. The playwright inserts his plants as subtly as the circumstances warrant. It is up to the director to point them up clearly, but without overstressing. The use of the scissors and the intricate play of house keys in *Dial M for Murder* are excellent plants, for they foreshadow things to come; so, too, does the unexplained lowering of the gaslight in *Angel Street* and its brightening minutes before the entrance of the psychomaniac. These are plants that build to the climax, making the audience sweat it out along with the victimized wives.

The Suspicious Character

Part of the fun in mystery plays comes from trying to out-guess the parties involved. The playwright does his job in dispensing the same amount of suspicion for each character. We must respect this controlled impartiality by giving emphasis to those lines of dialogue that incriminate or acquit by selective use of business or pantomime, and by carefully designed picturization in order to balance the amount of suspicion on each character. It would be throwing out the zest of the mystery if in their readings, reactions, or behavior the actors unconsciously "betrayed" the culprit. This is not likely to happen if the balance is consistently maintained until the final giveaway. In this regard, the director can spread suspicion beyond the demands of the text, if necessary, by subtle focus—through secondary emphasis, for instance—on a peripheral character in a scene of accusation.

DEMONSTRATION

Primary focus is is on a character under suspicion. At a vital point in the evidence the peripheral character reacts with a turn from the center of focus—a rise, a sit, or whatever is warranted by the circumstances. Members of the audience catch this reaction and, being secondary to the main scene, feel the pride of discovery. The peripheral character is added to the list of suspicious characters.

To keep an audience guessing beyond what is offered through plot development, the director can throw suspicion on a character by intentionally signaling his reaction.

THE SENTIMENTAL COMPARED
TO THE MELODRAMATIC

Often, greater dramatic value is derived from some plays by toning down their melodramatic qualities. Before pursuing this further, a few words should be said about plays classed as sentimental. Historically, this includes plays of sentiment of the eighteenth and nineteenth centuries. In this category are also the plays similar to those of J. M. Barrie and William Saroyan, along with television's splurge of "soap operas."

True sentiment has an inner vitality since it is backed by

honest characterization. But in plays of sentiment where emotion runs rampant for its own sake, tender feelings flow overabundantly. Just as an exaggeration of the bad becomes "melodramatic," so does an exaggeration of the good lead to sentimentality. For these overtender plays the problem is to decide when or when not to eliminate or tone down sentimentality. Since the emphasis or elimination depends on the same general principles that are applied to building up or toning down melodramatic qualities, the control of both will be analyzed together. But first, the problem presented by plays heavy in sentiment merits further discussion.

Sentimentality should be eliminated whenever the playwright has overworked the sentimental passages in his play. These are the embellishments, the "purple passages." Justification for not toning down these passages might be the director's desire to retain the flavor of the historic sentimental play. However, experience shows that in their revival, greater justice to the sincerity of the work is served when sentiment and "purple passages" are controlled to a degree acceptable to audiences in the spirit in which the play was written. The plays of A. A. Milne, Barrie, and Maeterlinck present the same basic problem, which rests on no specific line of dialogue, but on the sentiment contained within the scenes themselves. The works of Saroyan, Benavente, Giraudoux, and much of Tennessee Williams need the same special attention. The danger in sentimental scenes is that the playwright offers the actor a flush of gentle feelings comfortable for him to relish. When the text not only speaks the sentiment but more often than not overstates a character's feelings, the solution is to give the scene solidity, rooting it in a reality by having the actor play honestly and attack the emotion directly, rather than lingering over and "stroking" the lines.

The following rundown suggests controls in building up the melodramatic and sentimental qualities indicated but not fully realized in a script or toning down these qualities when overstressed.

	TO BUILD UP	**TO TONE DOWN**
	THE TEXT	
ELEMENTS OF PLAY	Emphasize story and circumstances	Emphasize character and idea
STRUCTURAL VALUES	Increase suspense through elaborating teasers; develop climactic scenes to sharpen contrasts; edit expositional passages when permissible	Keep actions and emotions in
	FUNDAMENTALS OF DIRECTING	
COMPOSITION	Stress connotative values of line, form and mass	Use selectively for emphasis
PICTURIZATION	Heighten and enrich	Indicate by suggestion
MOVEMENT	Stress action and mood values	Motivate in detail
BUSINESS	Elaborate for story value and teasers	Select for character value
ATMOSPHERE AND MOOD	Enrich through details in production; play up contrasts; reinforce by music and offstage effects	Blend within and between scenes; eliminate or subdue offstage effects
RHYTHM	Make obvious with sharp contrasts and tempo variations	Use subtly
	PERFORMANCE OF THE ACTOR	
ACTING	Intensify feelings and emotions, with heightened reading of emotional passages; maintain sincerity	Keep readings natural and sincere
CHARACTERS	Stress the typical traits; react simply and immediately	Weigh the matter under consideration before responding
EMOTIONS	Contrast good and bad with sincerity	Justify or motivate the good and the bad
VOICE	Use warm emotional tones with contrast	Use a moderate tone

SPEECH	Stress the vowels that bring out the feeling	Stress consonants and articulate the words to bring out the thoughts and in turn the principal idea
GESTURE AND ACTION	Think the action verb, then follow through completely with meaningful gesture and action	Study the source of the stimulus; reflect on it
BODY	Keep tensions strong	Maintain an easy bearing

CASTING

CASTING	Contrast types to strengthen particular character traits	Work against type

PART 2

Style of Play

STYLE is the *manner* of dramatic expression that author chooses to use. The basic attitude in the writing may be *comic*, the purpose behind the writing may be *satiric*; but in choosing the manner of expressing the satiric comedy, the author may decide to do it either *realistically* or *romantically*, to cite two of the fundamental manners of dramatic expression. Style, then, is the author's manner of expressing the basic attitude. In these terms, *The Lady's Not for Burning*, by the twentieth century author Christopher Fry, is a *romantic* satiric comedy, while *Volpone*, by the seventeenth century Ben Jonson, is a *realistic* satiric comedy.

Both styles relate the plays to the world around us, regardless of the time when written or the period in which localized. As such, they are considered to be within the theatre of illusion. The theatre of illusion, however, when compared to our world, is actually highly selective, or romantic, classic, stylized, naturalistic, impressionistic, and so on. There are other plays that relate more specifically to the world of the mind and which in their fashion create a theatrical truth—a non-illusionary kind of theatre—that is expressionistic, or surrealistic, constructivistic, epic, and so on.

Ultimately, style becomes the controlling guide to the manner of acting, the design and use of setting, properties, costumes, lighting, and sound, and the controls of the fundamentals of directing. Style sets the limits within which all phases of production are unified.

CHAPTER FIVE

Naturalism

The play that attempts to capture the actuality of life is called *naturalistic*. Of all styles, naturalism in the theatre most closely projects a semblance of life as it exists in the real world—at least as the artist honestly attempts to produce it on stage. To acquire a basis for directorial controls in this style, we should first observe life from the naturalist's point of view: the world around us consists of a series of events with little or no connection between them except as the observer becomes the unifying link; any sequence of events in a person's life does not follow a continuous line of development, but is interrupted by irrelevant details, various thoughts, feelings, and needs of everyday living; conversations include unfinished statements, divergent thoughts, memories that surface, silences, and so on; happenings are affected by or affect each individual; we are the products of our heritage and environment. From the naturalistic view, in life there is no order, no logic, no idea, except as we give order, logic, and idea to events and human behavior.

CHARACTERISTICS OF THE NATURALISTIC PLAY

Denial of Structure

Plotting means order, but the naturalist cannot plot his story if he wants to present a semblance of life. Therefore, we should differentiate between the story of a group of people as in Chekhov's *The Cherry Orchard* and a plot wherein events are planned in a carefully designed structure with major crisis and climax, as in Ibsen's and Arthur Miller's realistic plays like *Hedda Gabler, Enemy of the People,* and *All My Sons.* The naturalistic play appears to be a slice of actual life—a segment wherein we catch people and events at a particular period that the playwright selects. Chekhov's plays, Gorki's *The Lower Depths,* Odet's *Awake and Sing,* Hauptmann's *The Weavers,* Sherriff's *Journey's End,* Osborne's *Epitaph for George Dillon,* Hansberry's *A Raisin in the Sun*—all are within the scope of naturalism.

Meticulously Drawn Characters

Being the story of people, the major interest is in the characters, scaled to lifesize and inconsistent as is the nature of people. They are typical of their origin and locale, behaving according to their social conditioning. However, we must distinguish between naturalistic plays that *present* character and those that *reveal* character.

In the journalistic naturalism of Sidney Kingsley, characters are documented in their responses to given circumstances. This is different from the minute probing into characters in Chekhov's plays, where the people reveal their inward fears and desires—understanding what goes on within and between characters comes not necessarily through what they say, but through the unspoken thoughts, or subtext, made known to us by past or present behavior.

Characters are also more presented than revealed in social dramas like Hauptmann's *The Weavers,* where the mob assumes a strong identity through dramatization of its behavior under social pressure—a study in mob psychology. In the same category are the documentary plays which depict actual historical events selected from one point of view or belief. It is important to recognize these factors, since treatment of character influences the actor's approach to his role and the director's approach to the control of scenes.

72

Colloquial Language

The language is commonplace, resembling the language of everyday life. It is consistent and true to the types of people represented by the play: varying dialects expressive of locale and nationality, colloquialisms in speech, little or no selection in capturing the trivialities of conversation, broken sequences in thought, and irrelevant remarks in the flow of conversation.

No Openly Declared Idea

The idea or theme of the play is usually buried beneath the clutter of relevant and irrelevant details. Out of the entire play, however, an idea may be projected which comes about as a deduction from the facts presented. The playwright makes no attempt to mold his convictions into openly declared statements by his characters. Kingsley's *Dead End* presents the daily lives of people in a slum area of New York City, leaving us with the thought that an indifferent society can create slum conditions which in turn breed criminals. Chekhov's *The Cherry Orchard*, by depicting a group of people in their particular environment and circumstances, indirectly tells us about an era in Russia when one generation, gradually disintegrating as a ruling class, was incapable of stopping this dissolution while a new vital generation, formerly in serfdom, was asserting their rights and taking hold of affairs. Implicit in Chekhov's depiction of human behavior under certain circumstances and pressures are universal truths. His concept of the dissolution of one class and culture of people, swallowed up in the growth of a new awakened society, encompasses the forces of life that brought about the watering down of an Athenian culture, the collapse of an empire built by pioneering Romans, and the revolution of a disgruntled lower- and middle-class society in France.

Scrupulously Described Locales

The playwright strives for verisimilitude in portraying locales. His descriptions mirror photographic representations.

Intrinsic Atmospheric Touches That Effect Moods

The playwright does not create a scenic background in order to accentuate the dramatic action by its atmosphere and mood. Instead, he chooses to bring dramatic action into the scenic environment where the details of locale and time intrinsically affect his characters in their thoughts, feelings, and behavior: It is the chirping of the birds in Act I of *The Cherry Orchard* that inspires Varya's remarks, and the cold weather that makes Epihodov and others react as they do; it is the glow of dawn throughout the nursery that bolsters Gaev's spirits, and the dusk in Act II that creates a quietness and solitude among those present, reminding Lyubov of past events. Or in counterpoint to these, it is the party atmosphere in Act III, with its dancing, games, and noisy hilarity, that by sharp contrast points up Lyubov's troubled state of mind and moves us to sympathy. The characters of naturalistic plays have their roots in environments where the atmosphere is true to time, place, and condition.

A Varied Rhythm

The phrasing of dialogue and the organization of a scene are the result of character rhythms as they are affected by circumstances, locale, and atmosphere. Rhythm, therefore, is peculiar to the life depicted with all the variations in the characters' tempos of living.

DIRECTORIAL CONTROLS: PERFORMANCE

In the performance of a naturalistic play, the audience theoretically sees the play as life itself. Of course, to say that art can be created out of strict imitation of life is a contradiction in terms. To achieve the *seeming actuality* of naturalism, the playwright exercises great control in the selection and use of elements. In like fashion, the director, designers, and actors must exercise great control to achieve this seeming actuality for the audience.

Aesthetic Distance

Histrionic and theatrical expression is eliminated. Whether the play is staged behind a proscenium opening, on a thrust stage, or in-the-round, there should ideally be no aesthetic or psychical distance between audience and stage, since the audience is assumed to believe implicitly in the events unfolding before it. The illusionary line separating audience from action on stage takes on the character of a wall (the "fourth wall" in proscenium staging) through which the audience is privileged to peek.

Acting

Characters are conceived in their internal and external traits as products of their heredity and society, and portrayed without resource to theatrical pyrotechnics or conventions. Since the playwright catches only a segment of the character's entire span of life, the actor views his character beyond the confines of the play's circumstances. To understand him fully, the actor studies his character's environment: its culture, manners, mode of living, social and economic forces, heritage, attitudes, morality—everything that comprises an era at a specific time in history. In line with the idea of non-theatricality, emotional expression in many instances is suppressed, but projected by other controls (see demonstration below). The detailed study of the character's background (both in and out of the play) supplies the added depth and richness that give dimension to these scenes.

DEMONSTRATION

[Chekhov's The Cherry Orchard, *Act IV. Varya enters expecting Lopakhin to propose marriage.*]

LOPAKHIN   [*looking at his watch*] Yes . . .

[*A pause. Whispering and suppressed laughter are heard behind the door, then VARYA comes in and starts fussing with the luggage.*]

VARYA   I packed it myself, and I can't remember . . . [*A pause*]

LOPAKHIN   Where are you going to now, Varvara Mihailovna?

VARYA   I? To the Rogulins. I've taken a job as their house-keeper.

LOPAKHIN   That's in Yashnevo, isn't it? Almost seventy miles from here. [*A pause*] So this is the end of life in this house . . .

VARYA   [*Still fussing with the luggage*] Where could it be? Perhaps I put it in the trunk? Yes, life in this house has come to an end . . . there won't be any more . . .

LOPAKHIN   And I'm going to Kharkov . . . On the next train. I'm leaving Epihodov here . . . I've hired him.

VARYA   Really!

LOPAKHIN   Remember, last year at this time it was snowing already, but now it's still so bright and sunny. Though it's cold . . . three degrees of frost.

VARYA   I haven't looked. [*A pause*] Besides, our thermometer's broken . . .

[*A pause. A voice is heard from outside the door*]

VOICE   Yermolay Alexeyevich!

LOPAKHIN   [*As if he had been waiting for it*] I'm coming! Right away! [*He exits*]

[VARYA sits on the floor, with her head on a bundle of clothes, crying quietly]

The characters' inner thoughts and feelings are revealed not through their dialogue but through their actions. The behavior of these two—Varya's pretence to be looking for something, Lopakhin's failure to propose—has its roots deep in forces not found in the immediate situation. The past and the present guide the interpretation and ultimate control of the scene. Through Varya's actions—the manner of searching among the pieces of luggage and kneeling by the trunk, the manner of opening the trunk and removing articles of clothes, the way of closing the trunk on "Besides, our thermometer's broken . . . ," and her collapse on Lopakhin's exit—are revealed the girl's pride in her pretence to look for something, her palpitating expectation of proposal, her realization that he will never propose, and her final heartbreak.

With Lopakhin we come to know his innermost feelings: of guilt, through his self-conscious turning aside from Varya when she faces him; of compassion, in his determined approach to her; of embarrassment, by his rebound and attempt at conversation; of terror, pity, and self-condemnation, through his shivering when by the window in his reference to the frost; and finally of his release from torture by the call from outside and of his anguish for Varya as he stops momentarily on his exit.

"The careful elaboration of restrained effects" has revealed the subtext, the unspoken inner conflict between characters.

Delivery and Bodily Control

Speech between characters is on a conversational level without seemingly conscious effort to project. This also holds true for physical reactions. Speech patterns remain true to the feelings, attitudes, and cultural status of the characters. "It is all written down," Chekhov would say after watching an abortive rehearsal; "they are acting too much. It must all be done very simply—just as in life. It must be done as if they spoke about such things every day."

Bodily control is expressive of character. Since the inner man is known through his behavior, gestures and movements tend to be detailed and plentiful. The "studied carelessness" in speech and bodily control (the "mumblers" and the "scratchers") was at one time a popular convention in the naturalistic school of acting.

DIRECTORIAL CONTROLS:
FUNDAMENTAL ELEMENTS OF DIRECTING

Composition

The sense of existence of a "fourth wall" between audience and play suggests that there should be no evidence of compositional treatment nor any feeling that the actions are being played for the audience. Body positions help create this "closed-in" effect by relating to other characters or scenic elements, but not to the audience. Subtlety, indirectness, and variety are the keys to control: variety within and between areas; variety in planes, levels, and body positions; emphasis with indirect focus and counterfocus. Balance is asymmetrical or aesthetic to conceal regularity of form. Since a substantial portion of the drama lies in the subtext, the connotative values of line, form, and mass become a major control by which to accentuate the basic emotions of the characters.

In contrast to the Shakespearean soliloquies which are delivered out to the audience to make it feel a confidant in the character's meditations and reflections, the Chekhovian meditations draw the characters deeply inward and away from their own immediate world, and audience.

Picturization

Naturalism's concern with people denotes a vital interest in the interaction of characters. This means that picturization can be as rich and complicated as the needs of the situation warrant. It includes all the characters in the scene, whatever their relationship to the focal action. If they are unaware or indifferent, this state or attitude is picturized as much as the positive feelings among the other characters. Unlike the more selective control of realism, the naturalistic character is never seen nor treated as though neutral to the main action.

The subtlety of control in this style rests in blending the picturization with its environment, not composing it with an eye to impressing the audience. The audience is in attendance "by privilege." The subtlety of control also rests in picturizing the inner drama between characters rather than the overt statements. But in the plays of journalistic or social naturalism where character is more presented than revealed, subtextual inferences are not that demanding.

Movement

The needs of character or the demands of circumstances prompt a character to move. Fundamentally, movement of character in naturalism is motivated by needs and desires—a projection of the inward state of character. Because of this, emphasis must not go to the movement itself, but to the condition that motivated the movement. In these terms, movement tends to be small in extension, broken in execution, and unemphasized. The direction itself of movement relates to the characters and the scenic environment, instead of being executed as a technical control to keep the characters opened up to the audience. One problem here is that movement from the downstage planes, as the character turns away from the audience and moves upstage, tends to connote negative values in characters, which is justified only if appropriate to the moment. Conservation and selectivity, therefore, still remain important guiding factors in naturalism, since movement, as one of the valuable controls in delineating state of character, can be wrongly used or overused and lose its effectiveness.

Business and Pantomime

With people and environment playing dominant roles in naturalism, business and pantomime become two useful controls in establishing locale and atmosphere, and enriching character. The knowledge gained from preliminary studies and research in character and environment is here brought to bear in minutest detail. Costumes and accessories, hand properties, and manners of a period become valuable tools when selecting the most effective means of enriching or expressing a particular trait, thought, feeling, or attitude. In *The Cherry Orchard*, Gaev has his cape, gloves, and cane; Lopakhin, his watch and chain; Trofimov, his spectacles and galoshes; Varya, her ring of keys; Charlotta, her rifle and cards; Epihodov, his guitar. Gaev's manner of removing his gloves and handling his cane, Lopakhin's fiddling with his watch, Charlotta's juggling and card manipulation, Epihodov's guitar playing—these reveal a state of existence that creates depth to the picture.

Carried to an extreme, business and pantomime can become a "glorification of accidental detail," which may have fascination for an audience, but offer little illumination of character or situation. Used excessively or over-emphasized, both steal interest from the content of the scene. For similar reasons, setting or clearing a table, dressing, washing dishes, and performing other activities must be executed so that they are kept within bounds of the scene and not handled arbitrarily that they lose the sense of verisimilitude to their counterpart in life. There must be complete follow-through in actions of this kind, yet the execution must not belabor the issue. In body positioning, area playing, and general flow of a scene, the endeavor is to blend the business into the action, particularly when a trick or recitation, or such, is interpolated. The interpolation should be performed for the characters, and only indirectly for the audience.

Atmosphere and Mood

Atmospheric effect—time of day and season, weather conditions, locale and environmental colors, period mannerisms, and similar touches—are depicted in detail. Since the naturalist's use of atmosphere and scenic environment is an intrinsic part of the action affecting character behavior, its control becomes a challenge in a style which "denies" theatre and "seems to exist" in the natural state. The chirping of birds in Act I of *The Cherry Orchard* would definitely contribute a disturbing offstage twitter, annoying the audience to distraction, if it went on continuously throughtout the act. Sound effects must be controlled to blend in with character actions. The audience should not be aware when they begin or stop. The same holds for effects like the orchestra music in Act II of *The Cherry Orchard*, or the chopping of the trees in the final act. Enrichment and completeness in atmospheric detailing are essential, but the handling must be carefully worked into the dramatic action. Once the offstage effect achieves its purpose, and the onstage action draws the audience's interest, it is time for the effect to fade out. The same kind of control is exercised for background actions like the comings and goings of the party guests in Act III. The guests must seem to be always present—an impression that is created by subtle control in bringing them on during transitional scenes and fading them out as the intensity of the scene builds.

While the scenic effects may *suggest* the atmosphere, it is the characters' behavior that builds the atmosphere of a scene. A hot, sultry afternoon that has its effect on a character, suffocating him into inactivity and indifference to some vital issue, has meaning only insofar as the character, through business and other behavior, projects that atmosphere to the audience: gasping for breath, wiping off sweat, removing a drenched shirt, flopping into a cot, and so on—but selecting the business and executing it in a way that brings added dimension to both atmosphere and character.

Rhythm

Sensitivity, imagination, and perception are the attributes that bring substance to the life indicated by the playwright and capture the rhythm that is unique to it. This holds for any play, but especially is true in naturalism, where the dynamics of rhythm are even more specific to the influences and forces of character, circumstance, locale, and atmosphere that bear down on the immediate action. Rhythm manifests itself in so many diversities of character and situation that unless a fundamental rhythm characteristic of the people and the times is established and firmly maintained, the presumably loose construction of the play can result in a series of spotty and unrelated scenes.

DIRECTORIAL CONTROLS: PRODUCTION

Ground Plan and Setting

The ground plan, expressive of the dramative values of the play, must also allow for the variety and diversity of actions called for by naturalism. Without straining belief, a generally broken-up appearance of the stage—through use of variety in area, planes, and levels and irregularity of form—furnishes the means for this and allows for playing in depth. In the same way, the setting must conceal all arbitrary qualities of stage design, presenting physical surroundings that seem to be from the locale itself: interior scenes with solid architectural elements, exteriors with believable landscapes. A naturalistic setting may seem a contradiction in the openness of central staging, but by creating "pools of actuality" with suggested architectural elements, a stylistic consistency can be maintained that is readily accepted by the audience.

Properties, Costumes, and Lighting

Properties and costumes must be true to the life depicted, and lighting natural to the locale and atmosphere. This calls for design that reflects the characters' tastes. Lighting effects must seem to be motivated from actual sources—for interiors: lamps, candles, window light, etc; for exteriors: nature's own sun or moon, street lights, etc. This also requires a directional use of light, employing changes consistent with the action of the light source—movement of a lantern, time element from dawn to dusk, and so on.

Scheme of Production

Actually, the scheme of controlling composition, picturization, movement, and business is conceived as existing in-the-round, for presumably the proscenium opening is non-existent. This concept of the existence of a "fourth wall" has led to the belief that the naturalistic play is best produced in a scheme of production equivalent to "central staging." The concept has also been carried to the extent of placing the audience itself within the setting as a silent observer, and at times as an active member in plays where audience participation is an integral part of the play's dynamics. These schemes do not achieve any more reality than playing on the picture-frame stage, for whatever the scheme, it is the audience's *will to believe* that creates the ultimate illusion of naturalism. Although in the naturalistic style we are presumably creating life as it is, in fact we are doing no more than replacing *in degree* one set of theatrical conventions with another. Naturalism in drama and on stage is theatrical.

Realism and Selective Realism

If we consider naturalism as the style that simulates the actuality of life on stage, the term *realism* is applied to the bulk of dramatic literature that still maintains a close affinity to the world around us but does so with stricter arrangement and structure, in order to focus more sharply on the dramatic experience or the purpose in the writing. If the writer is primarily intent on social satire, like G. B. Shaw, or on dramatizing a philosophic idea, like Pirandello, or on character delineation and revelation as in O'Neill's *Long Day's Journey into Night*, he uses greater selectivity in his choice of elements, and arranges the material for the specific purpose by stripping away the unessentials. He works with clarity and economy in shaping the material according to his major interest. A comparison of much of the writing of Chekhov (the naturalist), Ibsen (the realist), and Shaw (the selective realist) helps to distinguish the amount of selectivity involved.

A wide range in selectivity is also found within the scope of realism: from the seeming actuality of O'Neill's *Ah, Wilderness*, Ibsen's *The Doll House*, or Inge's *Picnic* to the arbitrariness and stricter formalization of Shaw's *Getting Married*, Pirandello's *Right You Are*, Coward's *Design for Living*, or Congreve's *The Way of the World*. Plays where interest is primarily in the story show a greater degree of selectivity than is evident in the naturalistic play, yet the more the playwright directs interest to language (Wilde, Coward, and Stoppard), or to ideas (Pirandello, Behrman, and Shaw), the more selection is evident and the more arbitrary the quality.

Granted that choices are open to the playwright, the actor and director, as interpreters, cannot avoid the practical decisions required of them in the process from interpretation to performance. The actor must speak the word, make the gesture, and feel the moment; the director must reduce each force at work in the play into practical terms of directing and staging.

The following breakdown indicates the tendency in selectivity and control from naturalism to selective realism. The important thing artistically is to gauge the writer's control, and then to maintain an orderly and consistent directorial control of the elements to achieve the proper tonal unity and style.

	NATURALISM	**SELECTIVE REALISM**
	CHARACTERISTICS OF THE PLAY	
STRUCTURE	Loose story line, with little or no pointing	Highly organized according to major interest in idea or language; careful phrasing; plot meticulously articulated
CHARACTER	Fully conceived with different traits revealed as demanded by circumstances	Only the essential traits depicted; consistency to type
LANGUAGE	Colloquial and representative	Polished phrasing for meaning
IDEA	Implicit	Explicit; direct building of idea; projection of playwright's thoughts
LOCALE	Scrupulously described	Designated, with no detailed descriptions; not necessarily particularized
ATMOSPHERE AND MOOD	Intrinsic; affects character behavior	Not necessarily indicated
RHYTHM	Comes out of character	Organized in the structure of the scene
	CONTROLS USED BY THE ACTOR AND DIRECTOR	
ACTING	Subjective; "become the character"	Sincerity in expression but with refined control
DELIVERY AND BODILY CONTROL	Intimate; no conscious effort to project	Articulate and polished; conscious emphasis on language and execution
COMPOSITION	Closed in: not evident	Opened up; direct emphasis to point up speaker when main interest is in ideas and language
PICTURIZATION	Enriched, complicated; includes entire group; basic situation picturized; projected out of character feelings, attitudes, and needs	Confined to the pertinent characters in scene; basic situation not strongly picturized; related to idea
MOVEMENT	Motivated by character needs and desires; predominant in negative values; related to environment; shows clearly the thought that prompts the movement	Motivated by needs to project ideas; predominant in positive values; simple and direct

BUSINESS AND PANTOMIME	Establishes locale and atmosphere; enriches character; follow through in action	Subordinated to the dialogue; used to point up line of dialogue
ATMOSPHERE AND MOOD	Depicted in detail through character and setting which includes properties and lighting	No direct application to create it except that the suggestive quality in design of the composition heightens the required mood of superficiality through selection of furniture, ground plans, and compositional control in planes, open spacing, vertical lines, etc.
RHYTHM	Unique to life depicted; affected by locale and atmosphere	Formalized; evident phrasing, with pace controlled by line delivery

CONTROLS IN PRODUCTION

GROUND PLAN AND SETTING	Strives for verisimilitude	Only the essentials for the play's action are selected, and some heightened for theatrical effect through design
PROPERTIES	True to character and locale	Selected for compositional design within mood values of play
COSTUMES	True to character and life of play	Designed for effect of character on theme
LIGHTING	Natural to locale and atmosphere; motivated from sources	Arbitrary

From this analysis, certain conclusions can be made regarding the playwright's handling of character, story, language, and idea in the realistic styles:

Element	Action	Style
Character	Penetrate	Naturalism
Story	More plotting	Realism
Language	Increase value	Selective realism
Idea	More stress	Selective realism

The playwright's handling of these elements and their relation to style can be better evaluated by comparing the naturalistic control in *The Cherry Orchard* to the highly selective control in Pirandello's *Right You Are*. Both plays give the impression of being written in realistic terms. Certainly there is nothing unrealistic about the characters, situations, language or ideas presented. The difference rests in the manner in which these elements are controlled and in the approach to the reality of character, situation, and dialogue.

DEMONSTRATION

The Cherry Orchard | **Right You Are**

CHARACTER

Principal and minor characters are meticulously drawn. Their behavior is represented in relation to the social milieu—they are of their locale, conditioned by it and responding to it. They are scaled to lifesize, inconsistent as human beings are inconsistent. Their most intimate thoughts and feelings reveal their background, past influences, culture, future hopes, etc.

The stage directions identify specific traits of character necessary in the development of the story. Moreover, in the progression of circumstances, each character responds true to type, contributing a predeterminded point of view set by the writer. Signor and Signora Ponza serve as specimens to be observed, analyzed, and diagnosed.

STORY

The story line is drawn out of a series of incidents that explore the feelings and thoughts of character, some seemingly irrelevant, but always following the course of human existence. Indications of any carefully worked-out plot or design are not evident. Instead, we sense the observing eye of the writer over a series of events in the life of the people depicted, though the connections between events are sparsely sketched in.

Selection of the situations, stripped of all unessentials, is the direct result of the plot structure designed for the demands of the idea.

LANGUAGE

The dialogue has a work-a-day sound: colloquial, with superfluous and unfinished expressions always true to the character's manner of speech. There is no studied effort to polish the dialogue, nor take away its dialectic coloring.

Dialogue does not serve character coloring. The primary intent is to make it pertinent to the theme. Selection and arrangement pinpoints those expressions that reveal or further the ideas.

IDEA

The writer focuses on a segment of society and acquaints us intimately with its everyday life, hopes, and frustrations. The audience is left to make its own deductions regarding the thematic intentions.

The content of each scene contributes directly to the theme with Laudisi, one of the major characters, serving as spokesman for the writer at the end of each act.

Once the control of the fundamental elements demanded by the play is determined, it becomes important to be consistent in order to achieve unity of impression. Obviously, it would destroy the total effect of a play to stage the first act highly compositional and in the second overemphasize the movement and picturization implicit in each action. Style is achieved by an orderly and consistent use of the fundamental elements. Just as it is inherent in the text, so is it the director's responsibility to make it inherent in the staging.

Shaw, in referring to plays emphatic in language and ideas, makes the point that "there is no time for silences or pauses; the actor must play *on the line* and not between the lines, and must do nine-tenths of his acting with his voice." The audience's attention should be directed to the pertinent dialogue which becomes the stimulus to the audience's thoughts and feelings. Any laboring of mood values or strongly rendered picturized moments would only charge the moment emotionally and distract the audience's ability to participate intellectually. The keynote to control is *to keep the audience intellectually alert*. In group scenes the problem in staging is how to shift the focus simply and gracefully without excessive movement that may distract the audience. Compositionally, this means a grouping in diversified emphasis whereby each character can take focus easily whenever the text demands it.

The focus of the highly selective play on ideas—or on the entertainment value of language—has a decided effect on the actor's control within a scene. Since the playwright has underwritten certain characters or left some characters suspended, the demand on staging is to restrict picturization to the pertinent characters actually involved in the situation. The actors who are directly involved have no problem, but for the suspended character, it is important that the actor keep his objectives simple. Often the actor must create his own objective for the suspended character; but whatever choice is made must not take his concentration away from the main action. In a properly composed scene, peripheral characters should reinforce the emphasis and contribute to bringing the eyes and ears of the audience to the center of action.

CHAPTER SIX

Classicism

Classicism used as a term in the context of style embraces plays as divergent in time, subject matter, and structure, as Mac-Leish's *J.B.*, Miller's *A View from the Bridge*, Eliot's *Murder in the Cathedral*, Anouilh's *Antigone*, Sartre's *No Exit*, Ben Jonson's *The Alchemist*, and Sophocles' *Oedipus Rex*. Before analyzing the term stylistically, distinction should be made between the word "classicism" as a concept and the word "classic" as a description. A work of art may be described a classic if it has endured a history or is the product of a mature mind nurtured by the culture of a mature civilzation. More simply, it may describe an outstanding superior event in sports, entertainment, etc. Or it may be called classic if it belongs to the Greek or Roman tradition. Something may also be described as classic if it is simple in line, uncluttered in detail, with a strong feeling for form, so that in the theatrical sense we have a world based on ordinary reality stripped of unessentials. In critical usage, both "classicism" and "classic," as derivatives from Greek culture, imply many states of being, attitude, qualities, and characteristics. For example:

Balance	Logical organization
Discipline	Moderation and restraint
Dominance of reason	Obeyance to the unities
Emphasis on structure	Respect for tradition
Formality	Singleness of purpose
Harmony	Symmetrical form

Most of these qualities are summed up in the succinct definition of Pericles who said that the "classicist loves beauty with economy" (the head), while the "romanticist loves beauty with ecstasy" (the heart). This implies a degree of objectivity on the part of the classicist as against the subjectivity of the romanticist. Evaluated in the light of these qualities, we can also understand why the socially-oriented, realistic plays of Ibsen (*Hedda Gabler, Doll's House, Enemy of the People,* and *Pillars of Society*) are classed in the classical tradition for their tightly structured plots, economic use of dialogue, careful selection of actions, and singularity of purpose.

In the strictest sense, however, classicism is a style uniquely its own, with a specific viewpoint in portraying the truth that the writer wants to reveal. In contrast to the naturalist or the realist, the classicist presents life not as a depiction of life itself—whether detailed or highly selective—but as an abstraction from experiences that reveals the inevitability of natural law. The classic truth is the inevitable truth in nature that cannot be denied or defied. It shows man in his capability to debate moral questions that concern his well-being, where he allows no bars in the search for truth.

DEMONSTRATION

From A View from the Bridge by Arthur Miller. Copyright 1960 by Arthur Miller. Reprinted by permission of International Creative Management, Inc.

In A View from the Bridge *Arthur Miller reveals a law of nature that within man are drives, such as love, that cannot be enclosed—that a passion, like protective love, cannot suffocate the need of another's love to find release. Ultimately, he reveals the basic truth that man's instinct is for personal freedom.*

[The lawyer Alfieri, in counseling Eddie, tells him:]

You know, sometimes God mixes up the people.
We all love somebody, the wife, the kids.

Every man's got somebody that he loves, heh?
But sometimes—there's too much. You know?
There's too much, and it goes where it mustn't.
A man works hard, he brings up a child,
Sometimes it's a niece, sometimes even a daughter,
And he never realizes it, but through the years—
There is too much love for the daughter,
There is too much love for the niece.
Do you understand what I'm saying to you?

EDDIE   (*sardonically*) What do you mean, I shouldn't look
          out for her good?

ALFIERI   Yes, but these things have to end, Eddie, that's
          all.
          The child has to grow up and go away,
          And the man has to learn how to forget.
          Because after all, Eddie—
          What other way can it end?

An interesting comment on the search for stylistic control
is this piece of soul searching by Miller in the introduction to
A View from the Bridge:

> I wrote it in a mood of experiment—to see what it
> might mean. I kept to the tale, trying not to change its
> original shape. I wanted the audience to feel toward it as
> I had on hearing it for the first time—not so much with
> heartwringing sympathy as with wonder. For when it was
> told to me I knew its ending a few minutes after the teller
> had begun to speak. I wanted to create suspense but not
> by withholding information. It must be suspenseful be-
> cause one knew too well how it would come out, so that
> the basic feeling would be the desire to stop this man and
> tell him what he was really doing to his life. Thus, by
> knowing more than the hero, the audience would rather
> automatically see his life through *conceptual feelings*.
> As a consequence of this viewpoint, the characters
> were not permitted to talk about this and that before get-
> ting down to their functions in the tale; when a character

entered he proceeded directly to serve the catastrophe. Thus, normal naturalistic acting techniques had to be modified. Excessive and arbitrary gestures were eliminated; the set itself was shorn of every adornment. An atmosphere was attempted in which nothing existed but the purpose of the tale.

The trouble was that neither the director, the actors, nor I had any experience with this kind of staging. It was difficult to know how far to go. We were all aware that a strange style was called for which we were unsure how to provide.

The "strange style" they were struggling to realize is classicism. In Miller's play, though the character Eddie is depicted realistically in behavior and speech, he becomes an archetype embodying the concept of man pitted against nature's law that life must be given its own way. Through Eddie's specific actions and the all-perceiving eye of the lawyer, Miller objectifies the entire concept into a universal statement of God's laws. By focusing on the essential actions that reveal Eddie's struggle with his passion, the writer makes the audience "see his life through conceptual feelings." At the final curtain, we pull away from the action like the zoom lens of a camera to see the crushed Eddie in tableau in relation to his own people, his friends, his home, his town, his universe. Here is the affirmation of a truth seen in perspective to the total man.

This "conceptual awareness" is a major characteristic of classicism. While realism remains within the world, classicism pits the world against its destinies. It takes individual man, molds him into an idealization of the passion, and then struts him against the inevitable. The effect is quite different from the personal involution of the romantic mind. Unlike romanticism, the writer creates the protagonist not as an individual buffeted with inner sufferings and conflicts on a personal level, but as the concept of a passion. The Greek employment of masks was a definite help in depersonalizing character, whereby the statement of character to thesis stood out much more boldly. In like manner, the "conceptual awareness" may be brought forward through use of a chorus, in the Greek sense; or through a narrator as in *A View from the Bridge* or Anouilh's *Antigone*; or through self-analysis as in O'Neill's *Strange Interlude*; or through debate as in MacLeish's *J.B.*

CHARACTERISTICS OF THE CLASSIC PLAY

Strong Sense of Structure

The writer does not depict a semblance of life. He reveals a truth about moral law in an ordered life and makes his point relentlessly. To achieve this unwavering direction in building to the climax, he works by abstraction and selects primarily those events and behaviors that expose the passion within the protagonist which is in defiance to the moral law. Within this framework, the reality of character, dialogue, and situation has a definitely positive outline when compared to the diffused and blended line of the realists. There is exacting organization in plotting—a cohesion of all parts where form and theme supplement each other.

Idealization of Character

The characters are embodiments of the purpose they serve in projecting the thesis. Any probing into character is primarily to reveal background causes as part of the psychological analysis of a character's behavior. Each subsidiary character contributes to the gradual stripping down of the surfaces that mask the protagonist's passion, and each principal in conflict with the protagonist acts as a rough edge that finally lays bare the passion pulsating within. This process of unveiling the heart of a character by stripping off layer after layer of defenses is beautifully demonstrated in O'Neill's *Moon for the Misbegotten*.

Eloquent Language

The eloquence of language rests more in its importance to the context of the play than to its inner poetry or actual versification. It is not trivial nor colloquial as is found in naturalism. Often, it is compressed, charged with an inner energy that ultimately explodes into expletives that challenge the forces of universal order. In the climactic moments, language serves to create the deeply religious feeling of the situation.

Direct Declaration of Theme

Though it is not explicitly spoken by a character, the thesis of the play is implicit in the utterances and warnings of those who confront the protagonist as does the wife in *A View from the Bridge*, Jocasta and the soothsayer in *Oedipus Rex*, and the Archbishop in T. S. Eliot's *Murder in the Cathedral*. The Greek playwrights employed the convention of the chorus to state the moral law under question. This convention exists in various disguises in the writings of O'Neill, Anouilh, and Miller. In general, the writer repeats the different facets of his thesis as a running motif. This conscious effort in emphasizing the theme creates an audience that sits in judgment. The audience knows the ultimate catastrophe toward which the protagonist is driven blindly by his passion despite the signs and warnings around him. Even when the truth confronts him, he refuses to heed it, for the realization that could save him from destruction has been replaced by a fanatic belief that makes him a martyr in a cause outside the reality of the circumstances.

Indicative Locale and Atmosphere

Since locale and atmosphere do not intrinsically affect the characters' thoughts, feelings, or behavior, except as they are necessary for story progression, an indication of them is usually sufficient.

Dominance of Rhythmic Phrasing

The dynamics of rhythm are inseparable from the tight structure of a classic play. Phrasing and scene organization are not the result of character rhythms as affected by circumstances, locale, and atmosphere, but of the emotional demands placed on the characters in the unrelenting rise toward the climax. In plays with choruses and verses, as the Greek classics and Eliot's *Murder in the Cathedral*, rhythm is conceived in actual musical terms.

DIRECTORIAL CONTROLS: PERFORMANCE

Aesthetic Distance

The writer takes an objective view of his subject matter, choosing to observe actions and behavior by commenting on what transpires through an outspoken character, narrator, or chorus. Different from naturalism and realism, the spectators, though empathizing with the protagonist, are not expected to believe implicitly in the events; instead, they maintain an awareness of the ritual passing before them and, as at a religious service, are inwardly moved by the universal truth that is revealed.

Acting

Classicism is declarative. There is no hidden subtext to hint at by indirection. The subjective analysis of character need not go beyond the statements in the text. In performance, the single stroke does it, expertly selected to say what it must by inflection, gesture, business, or movement. However, the demands on the actor challenge his entire equipment—physically, vocally, and emotionally. Since passion is released to its fullest, but controlled by the dynamics of the form, the actor must shape his performance accordingly. He first analyzes the intellectual and moral aspects of his character, rather than the causes that made him what he is, and then evaluates them in relation to the theme, charting the character's responses in the progressive revelation of theme and heightening intensity of his passion—in totality, an orchestrated performance.

DIRECTORIAL CONTROLS: FUNDAMENTAL ELEMENTS OF DIRECTING

Composition

The guiding thought in controlling the fundamentals is to relate the form to the thematic values. The director searches for the single artistic statement that clearly delineates the author's intention. Compositionally, this means a subtle formalization in composing the characters to aid the writer's objectivity to his subject, but not made so obvious as to dilute the reality. On the same principle, the connotative values of line, form, and mass are used to underscore the text with the appropiate mood.

Picturization

The same basic considerations hold true here as for composition. The purpose of the scene, rather than individual relationships, guides picturization. Heightened critical moments—especially those where characters are in conflict with the moral law—are strongly identified within the scheme of production. At these instances a picture often assumes the ritualistic *feeling* (not the rigid pose) of a tableau. The opening of Anouilh's *Antigone*, in which the narrator introduces the story and characters, and states the inevitability of destruction for those who defy God's laws, offers an excellent example of a tableau related to thematic values.

The positive and evident use of space around key pictures also helps to etch the meaning of a scene. In the more abstract use of this technique, the setting itself is devoid of all realistic appurtenances and becomes an open space with a variety of levels when called for by the demands of the text.

Movement

In principle, movement stems from character needs and drives. This does not mean, however, that the reason for a movement is motivated only by character. The action may call for the actor to be near the exit door: To motivate the movement out of character, the director can create a need either from within or outside character. The inner drive can be the character's reaction to what is said. If this is not feasible, an external reason to move could come from business: crossing to the door to flick cigarette ashes on a tray near it or to get a hat placed there on entrance for this purpose. The reason to create movement may also arise from the fundamental design of text related to theme, but again in execution it must seem to be motivated out of character.

The explicit theme of a classic play lends itself readily as a working concept to be projected through a fundamental design in movement which adds another control in underscoring thematic values.

DEMONSTRATION

[*Sophocles'* Oedipus Rex]

The disasters that plague Thebes are destined to continue until the evil that infests the community is eradicated. Oedipus, the king, pressures to find the cause of this curse. From the tidings that arrive, he learns that the evil is within him—murderer of his father and husband to his own mother.

The fundamental design for the play comes out of the shift in the fortunes of man from conceit and self-satisfaction to despair and humility. An immense flight of steps, designed into an architectural unit allowing changing use of levels in the progressive steps of the king's downfall, epitomizes the the rise and fall in the king's destiny. At the opening, Oedipus is on the highest level: grand, prosperous, master of himself. As each tragic im-

plication bears down on him, we see his gradual descent from step to step, although at times he ascends as the obstacles diminish. Not until the end, when the tragic downfall reaches its depths, do we see the king on the lowest level, nearly prostrate on the stage floor.

Business and Pantomime

Business and pantomime are used selectively as further means of revealing and illuminating text rather than detailing aspects of character, locale, and atmosphere. The attention remains on the significance of the circumstances and dialogue.

Atmosphere and Mood

Atmosphere should not be enriched to the degree that it becomes important in itself. Moreover, careful analysis should be given to the kind and amount of atmospheric touches, because of their influence on the resultant mood. In *A View from the Bridge*, the street scene where Joe phones the immigration office is toned primarily with austere silence rather than the sounds of passing autos, distant voices, and so on. The silence around dramatizes the throb of conscience the audience senses in him. Overburdening the scene with atmospheric touches would dilute the audience's concentration and deprive the scene of its stark reality.

Rhythm

The strong sense of rhythm in phrasing and scene structure and in the emotional drive of characters reaches at times a degree of formalization. Careful orchestration of the interplay of dynamics becomes an important control in creating the ritualistic feeling for the more critical scenes. The lyricism and musical form of choruses in the Greek classic plays and in plays like *J.B.* and *Murder in the Cathedral* offer good examples of the use of rhythmic formalization. Ability to coordinate delivery, movement, and gesture is an important goal for actors. Training in the classical disciplines prepares the actor for the greatest demands of his art. Intellectual penetration, grace of execution, controlled sensibility, and exacting delineation can be achieved only by intensive and continual exercise of mind and body.

DIRECTORIAL CONTROLS: PRODUCTION

Ground Plan, Setting, and Scheme of Production

The fundamental design of movement related to thematic values has direct bearing on ground planning. While the considerations are thematic, the parts within the overall ground plan must indicate the specific locale required by the play, even though the final form may be an abstraction within the scheme of production conceived by the director. Specifically, classicism, which presents life in a way that reveals man in conflict with the inevitability of natural law, channels the director into a scheme that differs from realism. *A View from the Bridge* offers an example of the two manners of expression. One could interpret the play as realistic, with a narrator. After all, these are people of low income, living in a tenement by the waterfront of a rundown district. There is the living room used for recreation, dining, and daily household work; the street outside, with a sidewalk telephone; an area downstage, set apart for the lawyer's office. With the text as written the director could enrich the behavior of these people and bring out the routine details of their daily living. He could build up the environmental and atmospheric aspects suggested by the locale and depict the passing scene of city people. Schematically, he could have a full-stage facade of a tenement house, with Joe's living room reached by a low flight of steps. The street would run parallel to the curtain line. In the opposite corner to the living room would be the lawyer's office at street level. The audience would be drawn into the lives of these people grounded in the locale, but would have no other perspective beyond what is written.

Realizing, however, that Miller has written a work with classical dimensions in which he wants us to view the destiny of one man in the grip of a passion that defies nature's law, our imagination takes flight in other dimensions than the earthy confinement of realism. *A View from the Bridge* now becomes a work of heightened reality, not pedestrian realism. In this light, the scheme of production is conceived out of a fundamental design of a man sucked into his own whirlwind of passion. Rather than confine the playing area behind the proscenium, it is extended toward the audience. Joe's living quarters are on a raised area, enclosed by an open arc of the street that winds from down left to a larger open space up right that ramps off. At the downright extension near the audience is the lawyer's office. The phone booth stands in isolation down left. Schematically, three bits of reality are established surrounded by space. Joe's living room becomes a microcosm in a universe without bounds. The entrance into his room is at right. Whenever he stands or sits, directional lighting sculptures him out of space. At the finale, he defies his own guilt, community, and God's laws on the ramp at right. He dies silhouetted against the open space at down center, his wife sobbing over him, his niece and neighbors looking down on a fallen colossus. They hold in tableau in a tight focus of light as the lawyer at down right comments on the eternal laws of nature.

Here, then, is stylistic analysis that has inspired the director to conceive a control of all elements of production, design, and acting in order to achieve a dramatic statement with singular unity of impression.

Neoclassicism

Neoclassicism as a stylistic term in theatre usually designates the classicism of the seventeenth century school of French and English writers, which includes the plays of Racine, Corneille, Dryden, and Otway, to mention the more preeminent. Though these writers were inspired by root principles of the classical viewpoint as a reaction against the flaunting individualism and disorder in technique of their immediate predecessors, they were creators in their own right. Singleness of purpose and the demand for order and restraint guide their writing. The strict obeyance to the unities of time, place, and action found in the neoclassic tragedies follow the disciplines of the classic vision.

However, neoclassicism as produced by these talented writers of the French Renaissance and English Restoration is not an imitation of Greek classicism, but a style that bespeaks their culture, tastes, and manners. The overadorned treatment of language, for example, was a projection of the taste of the period. A highly rhetorical mode of delivery would be in harmony with this literary ornamentation, and the desire to impress the audience of the actor's virtuosity was probably an accepted convention, if we go along with the satiric thrusts of Racine's fellow playwright, Moliere, who has the presumptuous servant Mascarille in *The Affected Young Ladies* extol the "virtues" of his Majesty's Players:

> They alone are capable of doing justice to plays; the others are ignorant people who recite their parts just as they talk; they do not know how to roll out the verses or to pause at a fine passage: how can one know the beautiful passages if the actor does not emphasize them, and thereby point out when to applaud.

In many ways the neoclassicists epitomize the objectivity characteristic of classic art. These were writers who paid scrupulous attention to the aesthetics of balance, proportion, and "everything in its place." Classic art, however, is not without deep feeling on the part of the creator nor without intensity of passion on the part of the characters.

Transposing the concept of neoclassicism into stage terms, the structural balance in scenes indicates a highly compositional treatment, with a certain amount of prettiness in the groupings if we are to follow their taste for display and ornamentation. The relationship of the stage to the auditorium, together with the actors' sense of display, indicates a direct playing to the audience. Technically, this calls for open body positions and use of downstage areas. The emphasis on composition means that picturization should be negligible, though this does not necessarily signify a complete lack of communication between characters. In these terms, movement arises out of arbitrary considerations to gain effective playing of scenes outwardly toward the audience. As for pantomime, a studied and mannered control suggests a quality of gesturing simply rendered, and in the tradition of the elemental gestural art of the Indian and Kabuki theatre. These are conjectures based on literary and iconographical sources of the period. Most important, they come from the spirit and flavor of the times, as inferred from their visual arts, poetry, essays, philosophy, dress, theatre architecture, diaries, and etiquette.

CHAPTER SEVEN

Romanticism

In direct opposition to the classical way of living and belief stands the romantic. What the classicist puts into order, the romanticist breaks into disorder. The first codifies and weighs the consequences of action; the second rebels and soars through and above the confining conventions of life. While the classicist's inspiration finds freedom of expression within a prescribed form, the romanticist's inspiration finds freedom of expression only in the limitless unknown. However, the generalization that the emphasis in classicism is on the intellect, and in romanticism on the emotion leads many to think of classicism as devoid of strong passions and heightened emotional moments and romanticism as devoid of reason. In distinguishing between these two antithetical modes of conduct, order and form must not be interpreted as lack of passion, nor disorder and rebellion as lack of structure.

As with the term *classic*, the term *romantic* has variable meanings. The most popular application is to romance itself, where love reigns supreme and lyricism is the password to the heart. Another popular use of the term makes it synonymous with the adventurous past and legendry. Poetically, it is the embodiment of aspiration and idealism. Psychologically, it glories in the deep sufferings of the individual. Historically, it can be applied to an era of protest against stifling rule and pedantic obedience to form.

Stylistically, romanticism encompasses an assemblage of playwrights that includes Euripedes, medieval writers, pre–Elizabethans, Shakespeare, late eighteenth and nineteenth century writers, and within our recent history playwrights like Fry, Maxwell Anderson, Anouilh, and Genet. We must also differentiate stylistically between the romanticism of *Cyrano de Bergerac* by Rostand and *The Admirable Crichton* by Barrie. In the latter, the return to nature, the break from social restrictions and conventions, are romantic notions resting in a character's belief. The framework of the play, however, is cast in a form where the handling of language, story, and scene structure is realistic, in contrast to the romantic *Cyrano de Bergerac* with its free and lavish use of language, time, locale, and varied moods.

CHARACTERISTICS OF THE ROMANTIC PLAY

Flexibility in Structure

Taking our clue from theatre's standard-bearer of romanticism, Shakespeare, the narrative story line allows the writer to roam over time and place limited only by the needs of his story. Where classicism's compressive and explosive tendencies relate everything to one major crisis, romanticism free-wheels, using several subplots interwoven with the main story, each with its own crisis and climax.

Twelfth Night is an excellent example of this: the main story line of Olivia, Orsino, and Viola rises in and out of prominence as the other subplots fade in and out of focus: Malvolio's inspired designs on Olivia, Sir Toby's prodding of Sir Andrew Aguecheek, Sebastian's meanderings, and Maria's machinations, all intertwine with the main story. Character and emotional development are the measurement of consistency rather than passage of time, place of locale, or day-to-day logic in behavior. The disregard of unity of time and place, along with the anachronism and factual inconsistencies that abound in Shakespeare, is not an issue in the romantic world. Unity of action comes frm the account of the hero rather than from related, particularized actions. There can be many actions in many places at many times, but the story pulls together because it extols the deeds of individuals: the *Faust* of Goethe, the *Hamlet* of Shakespeare, the *Peer Gynt* of Ibsen.

Particularized Characters

The particularization of character is present in the sense of glorification of the individual, enchanting the audience through the strength of his convictions in the importance of himself as a free agent, unhampered by social restriction, code, or law. The Renaissance man who wanted to know and explore everything is a clear symbol of the romantic character. He attempts extraordinary action and is articulate about it. When he fails, he suffers deeply, and is articulate about that, too—often majestically articulate. By extraordinary is meant *above the ordinary*, not fantastic. The romantic writer delves into the character subjectively, but unlike the realistic writer, he has his characters articulate their predicament in language that lifts the moment above the prosaic. With the romanticist, exaltation arises from spontaneity of release; with the classicist, exaltation has a preconceived purpose.

Picturesque Language

One of the meanings of picturesque is defined as "evoking a mental picture." Where the naturalistic play details, the realistic play states; while the classic affirms idea, the romantic evokes feeling through imagery. These are stylistic tendencies of which we should be aware, meanwhile recognizing that language from the other modes of expression may also occur in each of these styles. The free flight of the imagination and the glorification of the individual entail a vocal expression that goes beyond the pedestrian. Color, sweep, flambuoyancy, lyricism, strong contrasts in imagery, sound values of words—through these and other senuous and vigorous expressions, the romanticist excites the fancy of the audience. Plays with a basic realism like Anderson's *Winterset* would lose their effectiveness if the romantic qualities in characterization and language were either denied or misinterpreted. The ennobling traits in Mio that drive him to personal revenge against great odds would come through as foolhardy; the transition into poetic expression as the peril rises and the tension builds when Mio and Marianna are trapped would sound like empty posing. The poetic extravagance of language is not a superficial treatment at the whim of the writer, it is an outpouring from the need of character involved in an action that finds its richest truth in poetry. Shakespeare's plays offer excellent examples of this transition from prose to verse when justified by the dramatic needs of character.

Implied Theme

In part, romanticism moves us by expressive language that verbalizes the inner feelings of character—feelings that come out of the character's passionate desires for fulfillment of love as in *As You Like It*, of power as in *Macbeth*, or of retribution as in *Hamlet* or *Winterset*. Regardless of the basic attitude, the theme of the play is implied from the action of characters and not from moralizations. Drives as ambition, greed, envy, love, revenge, and possessiveness are the antagonists that rest within character, rather than outside character, as do the forces of moral law and destiny (classicism), or of environment and heredity (naturalism).

Diversity of Locales

An adventuresome spirit is the temperament of romanticism. Events do not confine themselves to one locale. Freedom of release expresses itself in the use of several locales in narrating the story. Romanticism usually includes many incidents of physical action which tend to roam over many territories, extending the range of imageries.

Varied Atmospheres

Many locales indicate a variety of atmospheres which go hand-in-hand with the abundance of feelings and emotions in character behavior. The play of atmospheres is the color organ that accentuates, supplements, and gives visual statement to the play of emotions.

Dynamic Rhythm

The excitement projected by romantic plays ultimately depends on the dynamics of the rise and fall of tensions, vivid contrasts, sweeps of movement, and orchestration of voices which are part of a vigorous and positive rhythmic pulsation. Gielgud, in talking about acting in a Shakespearean play, says this of the music in sound: "This is what I mean about modern Shakespeare. You have got to somehow reduce it to a terribly fine point of truth so that it doesn't become just sound for its own sake. And yet you have to know that a great speech like Cleopatra's speech on the death of Anthony is written for the sound and not for the sense."

By giving careful attention to the rhythm and phrasing of line for sound as much as sense, the actor contributes his share to the rhythmic impact of the dialogue intended by the playwright.

DIRECTORIAL CONTROLS: PERFORMANCE

Aesthetic Distance

Naturalism's intention is to eliminate aesthetic distance by having the audience believe implicitly in the events. Romanticism, by its nature of expression and theatricality, creates an aesthetic distance and gains empathy by direct stimulation of the audience's emotions and feelings. This technique of gaining empathy is an important consideration in handling directorial controls.

Acting

"Actors," says John Gielgud, "are inclined to worry about the sense in Shakespeare, and to worry about the life of the character before the play began, which is one of the things that Stanislavsky talks a lot about. Granville-Barker once told me a wonderful thing—that realistic off-stage time did not begin till Ibsen. Therefore, in Shakespeare, it is no good asking what Portia's father was like, or whether Lear married twice and things like that, because *there is no life except that which is in the play.*"

The characters of a romantic play are articulate about their feelings and relish the telling in colorful language of imageries and metaphors. They can reach the heights of lyricism and by their musicality lift us with them. Again this puts great technical demands on an actor's equipment. He must have a vocal range and flexibility to meet the challenge of repressed emotions; and an agile and responsive body, grace of movement and gesture, to execute with ease the challenges imposed by text and period. The final test of good acting is to project the truth of the character, whatever the circumstances, and not the limited truth of the actor.

In a realistic play, the truth rests in the subtext and the actor's ability to concentrate on it; in a romantic play, the truth rests in the open text and the actor's ability to express it. The first is subjective in approach; the second, objective. Both demand truthful portrayal. Shaw makes this point about acting in Shakespeare: "Play on the line, and within the lines. Never in between the lines." It is evident that poor speech, inability to project, awkward, tight movement, extended pauses for reflection, and such, may make subjective acting acceptable but never objective acting.

An interesting observation about text and the use or misuse of romantic control in delivery and gesture can be found in the study of the nineteenth century theatre of sentimental dramas and melodramas. Here, the tradition of acting in the romantic style, in the romantic revival earlier in the century, carried over into the acting of plays with pedestrian plots, characters, and language. The term *melodramatic*, applied in a derogatory or burlesque sense to acting, actually describes the inconsistency that results when the mode of acting in a romantic style is applied to a realistic text with prosaic language, characters, and situations.

DIRECTORIAL CONTROLS: FUNDAMENTAL ELEMENTS OF DIRECTING

Composition

The outward thrust of romanticism suggests a bold approach to control. There is a flare of showmanship that can be complemented by aesthetically pleasing compositions. Levels, steps, ramps, stairways, balconies, or parapets when applicable to the circumstances add dynamic interest to the grouping. Where major events revolve around the protagonist, sharp focus and direct emphasis help build his importance and the brilliancy associated with the style. Generally, the sweep of movement signifies less breaking up within area and extension of actions over many areas.

Picturization

The director stresses the visual qualities of the scene when picturizing character relationships. The grouping of subsidiary characters in major actions can contribute significantly to the sweep and meaning of the design. Unlike certain other styles, these subsidiary groups are not kept neutral to the action, but are staged pictorially to project the basic emotions of the scene.

Romantic pictures like those of Delacroix, Courbet, Lorrain, Turner, and Constable are a good source for the study of effective treatment of group picturization.

Movement

The use of movement is readily illustrated by the following example: When turmoil within characters could be shown either by proper positioning or the amount and manner of movement, the romantic approach leads to the latter, motivating the movement as much out of the inner dynamics of a scene as out of the inner impulse of character. The emotional outbursts of characters and the imageries expressed are sufficient to motivate movement. The flare and abandonment of the style, when related to certain periods and characters, demands free movement executed in a long, sweeping manner. Whereas in classicism the vertical line is used to connote the text's inner formality, in romanticism the curved line, generously and pictorially executed in gesture, composition, and movement, connotes its sense of abandonment.

Business and Pantomime

Given the pictorial qualities and enlargement called for by romanticism, any detailing and follow-through in business or laboring in pantomime would only hamper the flow of movement inherent in its dynamics. This is particular true for the romantic play of intrigue, where dash and poetic extravagance provide much of the theatrical thrill.

Atmosphere and Mood

The vigor of romanticism should not muddy, diminish, or sentimentalize the story. Though the actions are dipped in atmospheres of vivid colors, they should not be inundated with striking effects of light and sound or startling background activities which can happen when enthusiasm shifts focus from the essentials of story to theatrics.

Rhythm

A strong feeling of rhythmic movement in all aspects of acting, direction, and production is the pulse of romanticism. The release into rich and full expression, striking contrasts, and exaltation of character epitomize rhythm at work in its most dominant aspect. Passion is strong, the pictorial is vivid, and movement has flare, because they are manifestations of a rhythm that moves freely up and down the scale in any tempo.

DIRECTORIAL CONTROLS: PRODUCTION

Ground Plan, Setting, Costume, and Scheme of Production

The discussion on scheme of production in reference to Shakespeare's *As You Like It* in the introduction indicates the wide range of possibilities in design offered by the romantic play. In scene or costume design, the aim is not necessarily to achieve period accuracy, but rather to capture the spirit of an age. The concept behind ground planning is to free the boundaries of the stage and to expand the romantic world of the play over the entire auditorium, so that the audience becomes one with this world. The structure of the Elizabethan theatre inspired this outward-reaching characteristic of romanticism. Today's thrust stage captures the same spirit.

Neoromanticism

Neoromanticism spans a period that can roughly be set between 1890 and 1910. Like its counterpart in classicism, it, too, was a repudiation of a prevailing tendency in artistic expression—this time against the naturalist, the objective scientific purveyors of the external world. Like the neoclassicists, the neoromanticists were not just imitators of the parent style. Romanticists like Maeterlinck, Rostand, Dunsany, D'Annunzio, Masefield, Stephen Phillips, Hoffmanstahl, and later Yeats,

Lorca, Claudel, and Ghelderode breathed a new life into the art of their time by creating a romantic drama of symbolism with a concern for the soul of man. They listened with a lyrical ear to the inner life of man. Theirs was a search into the behaviorism of man, but expressed beautifully rather than morbidly, exposing the soul gently as in the natural flowering of petals rather than the clinical slicing by a scalpel.

Characteristic of the theatre of the neoromanticists is the control of character, language, and situation in a way that mood and atmosphere are evoked through suggestive elements. Maurice Maeterlinck's characters in *Pelleas and Melisande*, *The Intruder*, and *The Blind* are spiritual abstractions symbolizing the struggle of suffering souls. Their involvement in situations and the manner of their speech imply rather than express feelings. Maeterlinck's belief was that what is unspoken can be as dramatically effective as the outspoken. His search was to push through the external and probe the overtones of words. His essay on *The Tragical in Daily Life* states his theory of "static" drama:

> *I have grown to believe than an old man, seated in his armchair, waiting patiently, with his lamp beside him; giving unconscious ear to all the eternal laws that reign about his house, interpreting, without comprehending, the silence of doors and windows and the quivering voice of the light, submitting with bent head to the presence of his soul and destiny—I have grown to believe that he, motionless as he is, does yet live in reality a deeper, more human and more universal life than the lover who strangles his mistress, the captain who conquers in battle, or the husband who avenges his honor.*
>
> *I shall be told, perhaps, that a motionless life would be invisible, that therefore animation must be conferred upon it, and movement, and that such varied movement as would be acceptable is to be found only in the few passions of which use has hitherto been made. I do not know whether it be true that a static theatre is impossible. Indeed, to me it seems to exist already. Most of the tragedies of Aeschylus are tragedies without movement.*

Though the movement in neoromanticism had in theatrical terms a limited run, it merits attention for opening up a new vista in dramatic expression which had its influence on later playwrights. The concept of evoking mood in the audience was the breakthrough to a new dramatic approach. By means of word imagery and the connotative value of sounds of words and their repetition, by veiled implications of circumstances, and by concealment in silences and concrete symbols, the Maeterlinckian play can envelop an audience in a melancholia of the unknown or an unfathomable fear. It can achieve in dramatic form Maeterlinck's belief that the unconscious feeling of the presence of personal death colors most of man's everyday behavior.

Maeterlinck opened up new vistas in dramatic form by projecting the inner feeling without creating an objective reality. He influenced Giraudoux, Claudel, Lorca, and Yeats, which in turn opened other channels for theatrical expression for writers like Beckett, Pinter, and Albee.

Maeterlinck turned the symbol to dramatic use. Thomas Carlyle said that "in a symbol there is concealment and yet revelation; hence, by silence and speech acting together comes a double significance."

DEMONSTRATION

From Pelleas and Melisande by Maurice Maeterlinck. Translation by Richard Hovey. © Stone & Kimball, 1896. Published by Dodd, Mead, & Co., 1911, N.Y.

[The ring scene in Act II, Scene 1. A fountain in the gardens. Pelleas and Melisande, bride of Pelleas's brother Golaud, meet secretly.]

PELLEAS   It was at the brink of a spring, too, that he found you?
MELISANDE   Yes . . .
PELLEAS   What did he say to you?

MELISANDE	Nothing—I no longer remember . . .
PELLEAS	Was he quite near you?
MELISANDE	Yes; he would have kissed me.
PELLEAS	And you would not?
MELISANDE	No.
PELLEAS	Why would you not?
MELISANDE	Oh! Oh! I saw something pass at the bottom of the water . . .
PELLEAS	Take care! Take care!—you will fall! What are you playing with?
MELISANDE	With the ring he gave me . . .
PELLEAS	Take care; you will lose it . . .
MELISANDE	No, no; I am sure of my hands . . .
PELLEAS	Do not play so, over so deep a water . . .
MELISANDE	My hands do not tremble.
PELLEAS	How it shines in the sunlight! Do not throw it so high in the air . . .
MELISANDE	Oh!
PELLEAS	It has fallen?
MELISANDE	It has fallen into the water!
PELLEAS	Where is it! Where is it?
MELISANDE	I do not see it sink . . .
PELLEASE	I think I see it shine . . .
MELISANDE	My ring?
PELLEAS	Yes, yes; down yonder . . .
MELISANDE	Oh! Oh! It is so far away from us! . . . no, no, that is not it . . . that is not it . . . It is lost . . . lost . . . There is nothing any more but a great circle on the water . . . What shall we do? What shall we do now?
PELLEAS	You need not be so troubled for a ring. It is nothing. We shall find it again, perhaps. Or else we will find another . . .
MELISANDE	No, no; we shall never find any others either . . . And yet I thought I had it in my hands . . . I had already shut my hands, and it is fallen in spite of all . . . I threw it too high, toward the sun . . .

PELLEAS	Come, come, we will come back another way; come, it is time. They will come to meet us. It was striking noon at the moment the ring fell.
MELISANDE	What shall we say to Golaud if he ask where it is?
PELLEAS	The truth, the truth, the truth . . .

[*They exit*]

The word imagery, sound, and silence, the implication of a surrounding threat, the unfulfilled aspirations, the concrete symbol of the ring falling into a deep well, the atmosphere of the deepening dusk—through these devices Maeterlinck creates the feeling of man's impotence before nature, in the case of Pelleas and Melisande the inevitable self-destruction of youthful love. The drama rests in the subtext, revealing the inner truth through evocation rather than direct expression. Where writers like Maeterlinck, Hofmannsthal, and Dunsany used spiritual abstractions (characters who inhabit atmospheres that are a refuge from everyday experiences), Chekhov made effective dramatic use of the technique by dealing with ordinary people and circumstances.

The neoromantic movement also opened new vistas in stage design and directing—the synthesis of space, color, light, music, movement, and the connotative value of words to express one mood. The productions of the art theatres inspired by the theories and works of Adolph Appia and Gordon Craig are a visual manifestation of the neoromantic style.

The atmospheric painting by language, the lyrical expression of the inner man, the misty environments, and the unfathomable circumstances that epitomize this style are in marked contrast to the strength and vigor of the romantic. Directorially, we should project the emotion behind the dialogue, the unspoken action. In subtext, this means that action and reaction exist in the *understanding* of what we say, not in *what* we say: "To get true action we must see through words to what is in your eyes." We have here the inability of man to communicate—one of the overworked themes of the absurdist writers. As for the fundamentals of directing, composition and movement stress the connotative effects, while picturization brings out the hidden emotional relationships of character rather than the immediate external appearances. To avoid is the tendency to immerse characters and actions deeply in atmosphere and mood to a point where souls truly become phantasma, devoid of flesh and blood. Softness and moodiness can be vitalized by strenthening the presence of character, the conviction in feelings, and the attack on delivery.

Rostand's *Cyrano de Bergerac* is an example of the new romanticism that flourished at the turn of the twentieth century. The work projects vigor through its substantial character portrayals and vitality in situations and language, and sustains it through the final scene set in the cloistered garden of a nunnery with the falling leaves of an autumn dusk and vestry bells reverberating in the background. The scene creates the full color of a neoromantic setting, as does its symbolism. It is the symbolism and the unspoken action that give the clue to the directorial controls to employ in reenforcing the thematic values of the play. The symbolism of Cyrano's return to nature is captured through his position in the shadows of the tree where the leaves fall around him, in contrast to Roxane who sits in the light of the setting sun. When Roxane finally perceives that it has been Cyrano's love that has touched her, and draws him out of the shadows, the gesture is too late: "In my life I have loved one person and lost him twice." The scene receives its strong vitality through the strength of the injured and dying Cyrano, who reaches his noblest moment in his final "duel" with prejudices. Thematically, Rostand juxtaposes the two uglinesses that were the undoing of Cyrano—the ugliness of his nose (undue weight given to physical beauty) and the ugliness in society (undue weight of prejudice that makes people compromise their integrity). Both are highlighted by reenforcing the commitment given them by each character.

CHAPTER EIGHT

Expressionism

The importance of expressionism in the theatre rests not so much on the plays that can be considered within this style as on the movement's influence on playwrights, directors, and designers. To the expressionist true reality is achieved most effectively not by selecting aspects of life, nor by rendering life in a certain way, but through his vision in expressing the *essence of things*. His aim is to transform the feel of things into pure artistic expression. This is only part of the total approach and deals primarily with the manner by which he expresses his deep feeling.

One approach to the expressionists's way of thinking is his socio-political credo. While the romanticist extols the rebellious clamor of the individual against conformity, the expressionist screams for violent resistance against a mechanistic society. His is an outrage against the forces that seek to dehumanize individuals. He articulates this through intellectualized symbols, hurled out in strongly emotional theatricalities preaching that society can save itself from destruction only through individual sacrifice and the exercise of love and understanding.

A second approach to expressionism is the belief that pure form itself, rather than the imitation or impression of the forms of nature, can express the *inner being of things*—the belief that the deepest truth resides in the essence of things. This avenue to expressionism seeks to go directly to the abstract meaning and make it the medium of communication for arousing the spectator—an accomplishment possible in the abstract arts of music, sculpture, and painting where expressionism reaches its purest form, but difficult to achieve in the theatre where the limitations of the body, voice, and emotions run counter to abstraction making it that much easier for an audience to interpret what it sees in terms of the real.

A third approach is to view matters subjectively through the mind of the protagonist whom the author puts into some state of aberration—be it dream, fear, nightmare, or mental abnormality—in developing his thesis.

DEMONSTRATION

Comparison of the three approaches to expressionism with naturalism.

Allowing that the theme of a play can be told in different styles, the thesis that war is hell can be expounded naturalistically through a treatment like R. C. Sherriff's Journey's End where we are made to live closely with the men in the dugouts, breathing their fears, sweat, patience, frustrations, and horror in the depiction of day-to-day life under fire.

Presenting this same thesis expressionistically within the furor of a socio-political writer, we would go directly to the essence of the "hell in war." Violently aggressive, emotion-packed scenes would dramatize hard-breathing, huddled figures crouched against a void, uttering terse remarks through their pain and intermittent screams: a flash here and there of mangled forms as an officer, spotlighted, drones the names of casualities while a film projection of tickertape running across part of the cyc enumerates the battles, the numbers of dead and wounded interspersed with market quotations. Topping it all could be the unremitting ghastly whine of a dying "corpse" caught upright with arms outstretched in the meshes of barbed wire.

119

Further along the path of abstraction, we might transpose these bits of form, flesh, numerals, and words into suggestive and connotative sounds, colors, lights, and shapes like those of rotting helmets, spiked guts, splattered blobs, and screeching wrenched mouths—projecting the feel of the "hell in war" akin to Picasso's expressionist painting Guernica.

Developing this subjectively, the entire scene could be the mental aberration of the protagonist hero—an innocent victim of the computer age!

Typical of the socio-political genre in the expressionist mode are: Howard Lawson's *Processional*, Ernst Toller's *Man and the Masses*, Georg Kaiser's *From Morn to Midnightt*, Karel Capek's *The Insect Comedy*, Elmer Rice's *The Adding Machine*, and Sean O'Casey's *The Silver Tassie*. These plays include scenes that can be staged to the limits of abstraction set by the actor's limitations. Film making with its flexibility in camera control and editing (montages, dissolves, multiple images, etc.) adapts more readily to expressionism.

Many plays called expressionistic are products rather of the influence of expressionism and, though they contain expressionistic scenes, are written from a different perspective. O'Neill's *Emperor Jones* is a realistic study of fright, granted that in the course of the action we see Jone's frantic flight through the woods distorted by his distraught mind. O'Neill changes his perspective in *The Hairy Ape*, shifting from the realistic to viewing actions from the subjective mind of the protagonist when he dramatizes the nonentity of "civilized" society in the Fifth Avenue scene.

This same approach is used by Strindberg in *The Ghost Sonata*. Only here we enter the souls of several rich bourgeoisie to see them as they really are. But before the change Strindberg views the action in realistic terms. Using expressionistic controls from opening curtain would only diffuse its thematic values.

Friedrich Duerrenmatt's satiric tragicomedy *The Visit* combines expressionistic devices with the grotesque, and uses realism in the two central characters, Claire Zachanassian and Anton Schill. But even in their realism they loom as strangely symbolic allegorical characters in a poetic diatribe on collective guilt, where the townspeople serve as the true protagonist. *The Visit* is a macabre satire on the spiritual corruption of a society. The scenes of the hunt, the attempted escape at the railroad station, and the ritual strangulation are striking examples of the power and impact of expressionistic treatment.

As summarized by Sheldon Cheney in his book *The Theatre*:

> Expressionism, in the larger sense, means expression of the artist's emotion rather than the depiction of the object exciting it; means emphasis on form rather than on the observed fact, escape from the limitations of what can be seen with the eye; means intensification, not portrayal of life; means presentative as against representative production, with consequent shift of emphasis (in the theatre) to creative use of the characteristic means of stage art, to movement, color, lighting, action, as well as words and their "meaning"; means usually the violation of actuality, the distorted piling-up of emotionally effective incidents.

The task of containing the essential characteristics of expressionism is like tangling barehanded with an octopus. Its self-generating energy refuses to be confined to any one artistic path. However, a breakdown of the socio-political expressionistic plays yields certain dominant characteristics that can be used as a workable guide in interpreting plays nurtured with the same intoxicating spirit.

CHARACTERISTICS OF THE EXPRESSIONISTIC PLAY

Calculated Structure

Plotting in the sense of the well-made play is nonexistent; the story line does not follow the conventional pattern of the realistic play. However, regardless of its psychological and emotional explosiveness, the expressionistic play is structured by a highly disciplined intelligence, eager to make an effective statement. The writer's commitment to propagandize his truth creates a sequence of scenes that builds his thesis in a direct line. This frontal attack on the audience's emotions comes out of a boldly designed strategy of working with disharmonics in circumstances, contrapuntal scenes, variable rhythms, recurrent thematic ideas, fusion of auditory and visual effects, and other means spiraling out of the central idea.

Symbolic Character

In place of characters with the unique life of the realist are abstractions of characters depicted with the various qualities of man to symbolize ideas. The character of the industrialist in Georg Kaiser's *Gas* symbolizes the destructive aspects of industrialization to the society of man by being portrayed as an impersonal, calculating, inconsiderate individual. As such, the expressionistic character has no personal history or ambitions, no personality traits or humanity, no inconsistencies. His wants, needs, and personality are shaped out of the concepts of group associations or collective personality—the steelworkers, the managers, the Park Avenue set, the clerks, the downtrodden, etc. With emphasis on the meaning of an action to thesis, the playwright shapes characters into symbols as in the medieval morality play *Everyman* where characters are statements of ideas, attitudes, or representative of groups. The exception to the symbolic stamping of character is the protagonist who comes into conflict with these forces. The clerks in *From Morn to Midnight, Insect Comedy,* and *Spook Sonata,* individuals in clash with the symbols, serve as medium of communication between play and audience.

Telegraphic Language

The direct attack on the audience demands a language that is terse and sparse, shorn of adornment. Thoughts are distilled into active verbs, telegraphing the essential words for communication. Subtleties of subtext and indirectness are eliminated in favor of lucid and overt statements. Often the language has the intensity and compression of poetry, and combines meter with sound value for dramatic effect.

Concrete Ideas

There are no subtleties about projecting the spine of the play. The intellectual conflict is made explicit through symbols of character or action that are readily understood by everyone. Expressionism speaks in terms of universals rather than specifics. In abstracting the essence of an action or a situation, the problem for the writer becomes one of selecting symbols of character traits, words, sounds, and colors that have identical meaning for all audiences.

Abstracted Locales

Locales are selected and designed to reinforce idea. The living room is not shown to depict the environment of the characters in their daily living, but to underline the humdrum monotonous existence of the protagonist against which he rebels as in *From Morn to Midnight*. Both the form of the locale and the actions depicted contribute directly to the essence of "humdrum monotony." The ultimate in abstraction is limbo, where "the body appears without a soul, or the soul without a body."

Effective Atmospheres

The writer creates atmospheres to enrich the mood of the scene, which in turn is expressive of an idea: the dulling routine of the office in *The Adding Machine* or the raucous revel and garish decor in the nightclub in *From Morn to Midnight*.

Formalized Rhythm

An orchestrated rhythm synchronizes actions of characters, phrasing in dialogue, scene dynamics, and elements of physical production. The homecoming scene in *From Morn to Midnight* is measured in sound and movement with the rhythmic precision of ticking clocks. The frenetic run and pursuit in Lawson's *Processional* is counterpointed with jazzy accompaniment. These rhythmic patterns and tempos can extend from the everyday rhythms of life to abstractions in sound and movement.

DIRECTORIAL CONTROLS: PERFORMANCE

Aesthetic Distance

Simply expressed, the writer lets the audience know that it is sitting in a theatre, and then proceeds to bombard it with every theatrical method available to arouse it to a highly emotional state of indignation.

Acting

The symbolic character exists as an abstraction of the writer's imagination that embodies his feeling about an attitude, an institution, or a class of society. The character has no other existence beyond this point, and may lack personal heritage or environmental influence; but this does not mean characterization without reality or credibility in the acting. The effectiveness of any portrayal, even the soulless bodies of the robots in *Insect Comedy*, demands an inner reality which the actor supplies out of his understanding of the character as a symbol and its relation to the theme. The text furnishes the clues to identity to which the actor gives substance in body, voice, feelings, and imagination. Ultimately, it is the actor's conviction that gains the spectator's attention. The fascination of acting in an expressionistic play is the demands that it makes on an actor's imagination—from playing a Zero to an Aggrieved Soul, from Goodness to Moneybags, or from Man to three contradictory Identities—all without other qualifications.

DIRECTORIAL CONTROLS:
FUNDAMENTAL ELEMENTS OF DIRECTING

Outside of the usual functions of the fundamentals, where the writer's objective is to abstract the essence of a scene, the mood values of the fundamentals offer the means to arousing the emotions of the audience directly more in line with the abstract arts. A demonstration of this can be made with the tea scene from Rice's *The Adding Machine*. But before doing so, the term *stylization* needs to be defined.

Stylization

The term signifies a degree of abstraction in stylistic or period connotation—a setting can be stylized by giving each object a romantic or classic treatment in line and form, or by using the roccoco motif, or by executing each element in the fashion of the Tudor period, and so on. In common parlance, stylization also means that the dominant character of an object is abstracted and exaggerated while the recessive characters of the object are eliminated. Under this definition a caricature is a stylization. Outstanding features like big eyes, protruding chin, or distinctive body build are given prominence over other features, which are subdued or barely indicated with the purpose of making special comment about the personality.

In *The Adding Machine*, Rice capitalizes on the common understanding of social teas as formal, conventional affairs devoid of any topic of conversation but the banal and trite. In this sense, stylization reaches a further degree of abstraction. In stylizing the concept of "tea partyness," Rice builds his situation, circumstances, and characters around the inane, the trivial, the trite, the conventions of deportment, the monotonous, and the repetitious through specifics in handling language and behavior.

125

DEMONSTRATION

From The Adding Machine by Elmer Rice. Copyright 1923 by Elmer Rice. Reprinted by permission of Samuel French, Inc.

[Scene 3. The living room. Mr. and Mrs. Zero are waiting for company to arrive.]

MRS. ZERO   There's the bell again. Open the door, cancha?

[MR. ZERO goes to the entrance door and opens it. Six men and six women file into the room in a double column. The men are all shapes and sizes, but their dress is identical with that of MR. ZERO in every detail. Each, however, wears a wig of a different color. The women are dressed alike, too, except that the dress of each is of a different color.]

MRS. ZERO   [Taking the first woman's hand] How de do, Mrs. One.
MRS. ONE   How de do, Mrs. Zero.

[MRS. ZERO repeats this formula with each woman in turn. MR. ZERO does the same with the men except that he is silent throughout. The files now separate, each man taking a chair from the right wall, and each woman one from the left wall. Each sex forms a diagonal with the chairs. The men, except MR. ZERO, smoke cigars. The women munch chocolates.]

MR/MRS. SIX Some rain we're havin'.

[The conversation continues in couples.]

FIVE   Never saw the like of it.
FOUR   Worst in fourteen years, paper says.

THREE	Y' can't always go by the papers.
TWO	No, that's right, too.
ONE	We're liable to forget from year to year.
SIX	Yeh, come t'think, last year was pretty bad, too
FIVE	N' how about two years ago?
FOUR	Still this year's pretty bad.
THREE	Yeh, no gettin' away from that.
TWO	Might be a whole lot worse.
ONE	Yeh, it's all the way you look at it. Some rain, though . . .

From a reading of the scene, we see that the characters become marionettes, the language a repeat of conventional phrases. To arrive at a stylization, the scene is staged first by working out movements, business, gestures, and delivery with realistic follow-through in action and thought. Having established a base, the next step is to eliminate superflous actions: a handshake becomes a straight extension of the arm, and up and down movement of the hand, then a lowering and nothing more. Boredom of a seated individual—normally expressed realistically by a depressed sigh followed by hand against cheek—may be told by a horizontal outstretching of the body; monotomy, by a measured delivery without change of inflection or tempo; conventional behavior, by having the men cross legs simultaneously and the women munching in the same rhythm.

The more the essence of the scene is staged through simple but telling line, movement, and rhythm, whether exaggerated or distorted, the closer the control approaches pure abstraction.

Composition, Picturization, Movement, and Fundamental Design

As in classicism, where the thesis of the play offers opportunity to relate action to a fundamental design expressive of the theme, the idea behind the conception of an expression-istic scene can be transmitted through a fundamental design. In Duerrenmatt's *The Visit*, Anton Schill's spiritual inability to escape his own share in the community guilt becomes the basic idea in the scene at the railway station where he tries to leave town. The passive lineup of the citizens parallel to the imaginary tracks along the proscenium line becomes as impenetrable wall of conscience, even though the citizens politely ask Schill to board the train to freedom. In the course of the action, while the wall of his own fears and guilt builds on his conscience, the wall of citizens vanishes as each walks off, leaving him alone. Idea concept has contributed the reason for the control of composition, picturization, and movement.

DIRECTORIAL CONTROLS: PRODUCTION

The expressionistic approach in directing—whether it be to stylize a scene or a character, to project individual wills in conflict with forces in symbolic garb, to dissect personality into several selves and present these visually, or to create phantas-magoric entities of attitudes—employs every element of theatrical technique to accentuate or enact the effect demanded by the text. Music, sound, lights, space, and other elements of production become effective instruments of expressionism and are inseparable attributes of the final effect.

Scheme of Production

The design of the setting conceived out of a scheme of production can project the essence of a scene in visual terms of line, form, mass, and color.

DEMONSTRATION

In the strangulation scene in The Visit, *the forward slow-action movement of the citizens surrounding Schill is spotted in a space delineated by light and shade. The play of colors, forms, and shifting radiations of directional light, indicative of a distorted conscience, intensifies the atrocity to be committed in the name of "justice."*

The overall scheme of production conceived in islands of space to capture the transient realities in the play is here put to use in a setting not indicative of a locale, but designed to symbolize the state of a collective mind.

CHAPTER NINE

Surrealism

Whether the artist represents nature or the world around him in its actuality or something akin to it, or whether he beautifies it, exalts it, or colors it with his own feelings, he is to all intents and purposes *looking at* nature. But the super reality, the sur-reality, comes not from looking at life but from *penetrating* the mystery of life, grasping its Mind intuitively, and then proceeding to create from this primordial and virginal center—an intuitive approach to art. It implies a belief that in man rest powers outside his range of reason, a belief in the naked primary power of the unconscious. The artist may attempt to reach this center—this eternal Mind—through the dream state of the unconscious, where presumably our true feelings come to the fore as images in our dreams; or through the innocence of the child-life unspoiled by the civilizing processes of training, social upbringing, and conventions; or through peace of mind—the Zen state—undisturbed by outside forces.

Whichever way the universal Mind is reached, we may understand it better if we say that the artist creates out of inspiration, but an inspiration that for some harbors the forces at work in the society of which he is a sensitive barometer. As he now gives substance to his deepest intuitive feelings, free of intellectual preconceptions, they take shape in dramatic actions and imageries that embody the temper, mood, attitudes, and atmosphere of his society. The artist's sensibilities, though personal, serve as censors of multitudinous kindred spirits. Beckett's *Endgame*—a dramatic embodiment of Soren Kierkegaard's "existential dialectic" of the death in life—strikes the tragic mood of his society in characterizations, relationships, and circumstances that are unlike anything we experience in our world. Nevertheless, the play presents a view of existence that is hopeless, sickening, empty, fearful, vain, and selfish to the ultimate of deceit and violence impinging on our own anxieties. The rhythm and imageries meld with the artist's intuitive understanding into an artistic whole that becomes its own meaning. Plotting and verbal explanations are not necessary. In his essay on Joyce's *Work in Progress*, Beckett states this view of artistic creativity quite neatly: "The form, structure, and mood of an artistic statement cannot be separated from its meaning, its conceptual content; simply because the work of art as a whole *is* its meaning; *what* is said in it is indissolubly linked with the *manner* in which it is said, and cannot be said in any other way."

Surrealism believes in the Kierkegaardian philosophy that "what really counts in life is within the life of each person"—the struggle that storms in us between our own life and our own death, whether consciously or unconsciously manifested. Beckett makes this struggle dramatically meaningful with the feeling of uncertainty that permeates *Waiting for Godot*, or the feeling of final dissolution that permeates *Endgame*; Arthur Adamov with the feeling of the futility of human endeavor in *Ping-pong*; Eugene Ionesco with the feeling of the "senseless, absurd, useless" in man's actions that runs through his plays.

Surrealism wears many masks which at times bears resemblance to expressionism in the surface results, but actually stands diametrically opposed in expressing truth through exploration of the essence of things. Surrealism—in whatever form it may take—explores the subconscious world in personal terms. Where to the expressionist the value of exploring the essence of things rests in discovering and then presenting the subject with universal meaning, to the surrealist it rests in the inspiration generated, and in the subsequent artistic outpouring from the deepest recesses of the id. While the two movements are at opposite poles in intention and viewpoint, their base of operation is the essence of things, which in the maturity of artistic expression of each come together in the form of abstract art.

The beginnings of surrealism rest in the attempts to find expression for the inner world. The recording of dreams and psychical automation proved logical starting points to probe the functioning of the mind and the subconscious without consideration of reason, aesthetics, or moral laws. Immediate results poured out as automatic writing, primitivism, and erotic images. The artist's fancy evokes thoughts and images apparently unconnected and at times oddly distorted, but joined in feeling by a psychic experience that makes the whole more intense than any one thought or image. The paintings of Chagall, Dali, and Chirigo capture this hallucinatory and metaphysical world in which recognizable objects and personalities, distorted or not, assume added and hitherto unknown dimensions by being placed in other surroundings than normally associated with them: townsfolk floating over roofs, a watch melting over a stone wall, or architectural settings within body viscera. This technique of placing the common in uncommon relations is carried into the theatre and motion pictures. In Jean Cocteau's *Orphée*, a white horse is stabled in a living room and a disembodied head floats in space to a pedestal and speaks. In Saroyan's *Jim Dandy*, snow falls in the quiet of a library; in Bergman's film *Wild Strawberries*, a coffin rests starkly overturned on an empty street. The fascinating, awe-inspiring atmosphere created by the surrealistic approach reaches its fullest expression in the fluid medium of the motion pictures where camera techniques and film editing permit the imagination to roam free of all restrictions except those imposed by the limits of imagination itself. In many ways, surrealism is the manifestation of the romanticist at liberty in the inner world of the mind and the subconscious, as in Fellini's film *8½*, where he attempts to capture the artist's creative efforts in the very process of creation. In its more elusive stage, surrealism spreads into mysticism and orientalism.

CHARACTERISTICS OF THE SURREALISTIC PLAY

Irrational Structure

The relationship of cause to effect vanishes into illogical movements of actions that find coherence, however, through an inner rhythm brought to the experience by the artist. Unlike the linear development in a realistic play, with its forward movement through suspense brought about by prior events, the forward movement here is achieved through the fascination engendered by the immediate scene and the play of contrasts and counterpoints from action to action, which stimulate curiosity and appetite for what follows.

Character without Roots

The insubstantial quality that characterizes the inner world of the subconscious can only produce embodiments of feelings and attitudes. Surrealistic characters are such embodiments. They do not have an individual history or future. They exist in the immediate present, and their behavior can only be evaluated in terms of their present action and thought. Their behavior is neither consistent nor inconsistent to character, because either condition signifies a knowledge of the past and a prophesy of the future—neither of which exists in the surrealistic world. Things just *are*; the entire meaning is in the *being*. With no roots except in the being, characters have compulsion to define their presence, drives, and concepts in the scheme of things. In this sense they are metaphysical rather than philosophical, which is the accumulation of wisdom that comes directly from experience in the world outside.

Evocative Language

The meaning is not in the dictionary definition of the words nor in the common parlance where overuse has debilitated them, nor even in the single phrase. It lies in a poetical juxtaposition and a new association that evoke feelings, meanings, and thoughts beyond those usually invoked by any one phrase. The problem for the writer is how to communicate the intuitive when confronted with the limitation imposed by words.

Idea through the Oneness of Concept and Form

Samuel Beckett states the artistic intention of surrealism in the quotation at the beginning of this chapter.

Unspecified Locale and Atmosphere

These are also inseparable components of the whole meaning. The bare interior with grey light in Beckett's *Endgame* or a country road with a tree in his *Waiting for Godot* are localities and atmospheres that exist only in the context of the plays.

Inner Rhythm

As content and form are meant to be one, so rhythm is meant to be an inseparable component of the meaning. The shifting form of structure, the unrooted characters, the evocative language, and the intuitive idea have meaning only as they complement each other and are given coherence through the deepest feelings of the writer—feelings that merge into a basic rhythm.

DIRECTORIAL CONTROLS: PERFORMANCE

Aesthetic Distance

The communication between the surrealistic play and the audience rests strongly on a personal level. While for one member of the audience it may be an enigma estranging him, for another it may prove a soul-searching experience. This same personal relationship exists for playwright and director. The director's intuition and intellect must work together in reaching out and experiencing the initial inspiration of the writer. He must "get the feel" of it and work from there. Unquestionably, the director should be in complete harmony and sympathy with the "feel" of the play, realizing at the same time the many nuances in attitude interposed by personal prejudices.

Acting

The dilemma for the actor lies in the search for some clearly defined objective to act on. An actor cannot act out pure feeling without sensing an inadequacy and experiencing an empty, generalized state that lacks truth. He cannot just hate; he acts on an attitude or state of mind toward some condition or person and projects what is interpreted as hate. He cannot act love; his concern, respect, peace of mind, and readiness to assist sum up the fact that he loves the person. To project feelings of hopelessness, weariness, loneliness, fearfulness, the actor must first answer "hopeless of what ?", "weary of what ?", "lonely in what respect ?", "fearful of what ?" The actor and director may intuitively sense the feeling of the moment, but to act on this, an objective must be worked out that relates to the world of the play, regardless of how intangible or enigmatic it is. In the final analysis, the work must pull together toward the feeling intuitively interpreted by the director, whose responsibility it is to generate the right climate for cooperative and creative work. If ever a style needed harmony and sympathy of understanding between actors, directors, and designers, it is surrealism. Without this rapport, the intent of the play will be as diverse as the individuals involved.

DIRECTORIAL CONTROLS: FUNDAMENTAL ELEMENTS OF DIRECTING

A dilemma also exists for the director in staging the surrealistic play. Unlike the writer who evokes states of being and feelings through indication and suggestion, the director must project these through the explicit use of the fundamentals. With text always serving as guide, use is made of the fundamentals to accentuate the special feeling implicit in each scene. Primary consideration is given the connotative values of composition, movement, and rhythm. Insights into the deepest recesses of the subconscious guide picturization. In this area, advantage is taken of visual images—such as those that sharply define the juxtaposition of objects not usually associated together. This adds a dimension and revelation not implicit in each element separately.

For example, a rocking chair may be associated with home, parentage, warmth, comfort; a field of oats with heritage, abundance, fertility. But a rocking chair dominant in a field of oats creates feelings of emptiness, visions of heritage left behind, and other similar associations that come from one's own personal past. The atmosphere set by snow falling in the library in Saroyan's *Jim Dandy* may for some stir up memories of Christmas cheer—of comfort, warmth, and fellowship; for others, it may imply lonely nights in cold, dreary rooms. Similarly, on a character basis, the person assumes hitherto unknown dimensions by placing him in a different surrounding than that in which he is known: an acquaintance met only at cocktail parties is seen in his professional environment; another known only in the business world is seen at home mowing his lawn. These are within the average experience, but in the substrata imagination of the surrealist, startling atmospheres are achieved through unexpected juxtapositions—an example is the Bishop in Genet's *The Balcony*, sporting in the brothel dressed in ceremonial garb. As for business, the search is for ideas that evoke the proper feelings and mental imageries to sharpen an audience's responses, as the repetitive business of Clov climbing the stepladder and looking out the windows in *Endgame*. Ideas for business may be found in the literal follow-through of active verbs and in the contradictions between overt meaning of a line and the accompanying action.

The challenge is to bring understanding to the amorphous,

mystical tendencies inherent in the style, and to do this dramatically within the context of the play.

DIRECTORIAL CONTROLS: PRODUCTION

Architectural solidity, logical relationship of areas, and realistic motivation of light and sound are wiped out by the free-playing imagination, which accepts no physical boundaries except those that are set down by the play's intention.

CHAPTER TEN

Epic Realism

Epic realism, more commonly known as epic theatre, implies a special method of acting and staging that cannot be discussed separately from its foremost pioneer, Berthold Brecht, who in practice was not necessarily bound by his own proclaimed theories. In *Letter to an Actor*, Brecht writes: "But for us, since we are making an attempt to change human nature, it's important to find ways to present that aspect of humanity which it seems could be changed by the intervention of society." To Brecht this meant an examination of the truth in his contemporary world: throwing the spotlight on ethics, politics, and economics, and presenting them with theatrical excitement for the stimulation of the intellect.

Brecht's theatre frankly accepts the reality of the platform and production, as well as the reality of the play—a narrative to be listened to, to be stimulated by, and to get excited over, but not to be mesmerized by it. The Brechtian theatre wants the audience to be familiar with its working parts so that interest centers on the meaning. It accepts the open relationship with the audience, whereas the realistic theatre, the "theatre of illusion," denies it.

Epic realism is logical, reasonable, and demonstrative. It has a social point to make, and it does so in episodes that are compressed histories of events selected meaningfully to demonstrate the theme. Brecht first prepares you for what he is going to say through a narrator or a sign of some kind. Next, he says it by dramatizing an event. And frequently he sums it up through snatches of song with musical accompaniment that often play counter to the mood. The intention is to awaken you to the significance of the events and so keep you objective to events—in the words of Brecht, "to alienate" you. Plays like his *Mother Courage, The Good Woman of Setzuan*, and *The Caucasian Chalk Circle*, Anderson and Weill's *Lost in the Stars*, and Bolt's *A Man for All Seasons* come within the intention of epic realism. The "alienation effects" of narration, song, music, staging, and acting are there to awaken the audience to discovering new truths. However, purposely or not, epic realism in performance actually heightens reality through the very unmasking of the artifices of theatre. It involves the audience emotionally through the actors' intense commitment to presenting the core of meaning of each event.

In a larger perspective, the manner of expression of epic realism is in the tradition of classicism. Thematically, however, its concern is the social world as against the moral institutions of classicism. It sees through the eyes of the sociologist, not the theologian; its interest is stronger in collective man than in mankind, in social ethics than in moral ethics. In theatrical convention, the narrator takes over the responsibilities of the classic chorus—narrating, commenting, and moralizing in verse, song, music, or dance. Dramatically, its focus is on the essential in thought, action, or object. Symbolically, it unmasks the symbol, using it openly as the periactoi of the Greek theatre—the paper disc does not pretend to be the moon; the way it is placed declares it to be simply a symbol of the moon. In its frank use of stage area and follow-through of actions, epic realism disregards space and time.

CHARACTERISTICS OF THE EPIC REALISTIC PLAY

Episodic in Structure

The main theme links episode to episode by the chronicle device of narrating the story. Epic realism carries no continuous plot equivalent to the well-made play, where each scene propels the action forward to crises and climax. In line with Brecht's belief in alienating the audience, structure comes out of a system of interruptions which generates excitement and tension as against the dramatic device of suspense in the conventional play.

In *The Good Woman of Setzuan*, Brecht shows that goodness cannot exist under the present condition of society by narrating the account of a prostitute with goodness in her heart who, in order to safeguard the source from which bounty is dispensed, must protect it with the hard impersonal facts of business economy. Brecht drives the point home by:

> selecting episodes to demonstrate her good actions and later countermanding these with business tactics;

> the dramatic device of a mask to symbolize the factual businessman;

> narration to keep us informed with the progress in illustrating the theme;

> snatches of song and orchestral interpolations to interrupt and comment on or highlight significant ideas.

Brecht creates no element of suspense, since that would shift the interest to the outcome rather than the immediate event. For the same reason, the dynamics of each scene are not forced toward some ulterior goal other than making the present moment interesting.

Stylized Characters

The characters are stylized in the sense that the traits and dimensions are drawn from aspects and personalities in society that are evaluated by their relationship to the theme. This process selects the dominant traits in line with the main theme and eliminates the superfluous. Characterization thus becomes social caricature and not the individual portraiture found in the naturalistic and realistic styles. The expressionistic influence can be seen in identifying characters by their trade or position in life. But unlike the expressionistic character or figure, the character of the epic realist has social identity giving him a smattering of soul.

Concise Language

The principle behind selectivity remains consistent for all elements of playwriting and production, which is to sift out the superfluous and hold on to the essential, so that thought and event are presented with absolute clarity. Trivialities and colloquialisms find no place with a writer whose principal concern is social awakening. Declarative statements, exacting versification, are used intentionally for what they accomplish in communicating information. In phrasing the dialogue, the playwright makes use of the gesture in the spoken word, as in the Bible: not "pluck out the eye which offends you," but "if your eye offends you, pluck it out." It is a language that is formalized, yet natural; staccato, yet fluent; strong, yet supple.

The epic realist compresses events down to their essentials, which in most cases means to compress the most meaning into the fewest words. This explains the frequent use of proverbs and epigrams found in dialogue sequences as well as in the soliloquies.

Ideas in Packaged Form

Brecht's artistry deserves admiration for his ability to compress a history, a biography, or a social climate into one basic situation in which the epigrammatic use of dialogue and the expressive use of pantomime open the door to a world of information. A typical scene is scene two in *The Caucasian Chalk Circle* in which Simon, the soldier, proposes to Grusha, the servant. Brecht creates in capsule form the span of time that covers courtship, proposal, and engagement. The scene is

141

sparse in dialogue, but pregnant in meaning. There is perception and understanding of individual and social behavior, and, in this situation, the anxieties and fears of loved ones separated in times of violence.

Indicative Locales and Atmospheres

The text describes what is necessary for examination of the action; and the method of staging, inseparable from the style of writing, designates the design in relation to the frankly open space of the stage. In demonstrating how the relatives exploit the goodness in Shun-te in *The Good Woman of Setzuan*, Brecht places the action in the tobacco shop, which is represented only by the essentials necessary to point up its social meaning.

Musically Scored Rhythms

In collaboration with his composer, Brecht carries his feeling for musicality into the play. Each dramatic episode, scored in harmony or in counterpoint, is equivalent to a stanza in an epic poem. Rhythmically, the pulsations of a Brechtian scene arise out of opposition: attraction and repulsion, tenderness and horror. The two contrary impulses create tensions, which in turn create the dynamics of the scene.

DIRECTORIAL CONTROLS: PERFORMANCE

Aesthetic Distance

Brecht's theory of alienation and insistence that the audience be kept aware of the theatrical surroundings, whether in play-structuring, acting, or production, makes his epic theatre the antithesis of the naturalistic or realistic theatre. The epic theatre accepts the open relationship with the audience, while the realistic theatre denies it. How this "distancing" of the audience is achieved is clearly documented by Brecht the writer, in the composition of his plays, and by Brecht the director, in his staging.

In play-structuring, he achieves distance by narrating a series of events from a past and distant locale in order to avoid the the kind of association and emotional involvement that happens when events have immediate significance. Then, by familiarizing his audience with the story, he eliminates suspense so that each scene is accepted for its immediate interest, and not for what is to develop; and lastly, he interrupts actions with song, music, dance, narration, and so forth. In production, he achieves distance by the exposure of all instruments and techniques; and in acting, by "presenting" rather than "living" a character.

Acting

In Brechtian terms, the actor must have a militant social viewpoint that shows through in his attitude toward the character he is presenting. This attitude, this criticism of the character, is built into the stylization, which completes the final portraiture of the character. The characters are portrayals not of individuals, but of collective man as a specific force in society. The actor searches for those gestures that characterize the collective man and in turn presents him through gesture. "All action," says Brecht, "involves gesture." And his theatre "takes everything from gesture" because it is a theatre of action. In action, the important thing is the characters' attitudes toward each other. "This," Brecht goes on, "is the province of gesture. This attitude of the body, vocal intonation, and facial expression are determined by a *social gesture*: that is, the characters insult each other, compliment each other, teach each other, etc. Among the attitudes of people to each other there even belong those that seem to be quite private, like utterances of bodily pain in sickness, or of religion."

This emphasis on gesture makes the Brechtian actor's job one of *presenting* character rather than *pretending to be*. Again Brecht comments: "To go from the mere copy to the image, the actor must look at people as though they were showing him how to do what they were doing; in brief, as though they were telling him to *reflect* in what they were doing." It is equivalent to what a director does when indicating the behavior of a character to an actor. The need for the director to explain a gesture through action throws the focus on the technique of execution and brings about a delineation of the gesture itself, unadulterated by any other consideration. The action of gesture-to-gesture becomes a choreography of movement. As Brecht puts it: "A theatre that takes everything from gesture cannot do without choreography. The mere elegance of a movement and the charm of an ensemble are alienations, and pantomime is an aid to the plot."

Awareness of form, in other words, is a way of distancing the audience. The focus on "gestural acting" is akin to the formalized movement of the Kabuki actor of the Chinese theatre, which in fact had a strong influence on Brecht's practice. The Brechtian concept of presenting character is no different from the kind of acting required by the *commedia dell' arte*, where the comedians "perform" actions on an open stage. Successful acting in the realistic style is achieved when the actor becomes one with his role, when he identifies with it. "He was the character" become the highest words of praise. Diametrically opposed to this is "epic" acting, where the actor never "loses" himself in his role, but remains detached—commenting, criticizing, analyzing.

Brecht's approach to rehearsals helped the actor to acquire the desired perspective and understanding of himself and his fellow actors. He would have his actors exchange roles during rehearsals, play roles of the opposite sex, or read out the directions.

The narrational technique of plotting the sequence of events that have happened to the characters also aids the actor's objectivity to his role. The concise episodic control of scenes, beaded one to the other, is conducive to demonstration by the actor who assumes the role of delivering an illustrated lecture—now signifying an important thought, now strengthening an important relationship, and now entering into the spirit of a scene to demonstrate a meaning. The "epic" actor never disguises the artistry that is his through study and rehearsal. The idea of spontaneity, of its "happening for the first time," is a gimmick of the "realistic" theatre. In this regard, some will add that the "epic" theatre is the truer theatre, and the more immediate, for it declares what it is doing without pretensions.

DIRECTORIAL CONTROLS: FUNDAMENTAL ELEMENTS OF DIRECTING

Composition

Characteristic of Brechtian staging is the extreme attention given to the compositional control of each moment in a scene. The spatial feeling of the setting, brilliantly exposed in white light surrounding real property, and the placement of the actors to create an effective composition of the whole, are a means of "distancing" an audience. Whenever beauty of form is pushed forward, the result is greater alienation from the emotions active in a scene and a shift toward the significance of what is being said. The objective is to achieve a union of form and content—compositions that are vital and expressive and that incorporate the feeling of the scene. Technically, this means compositional control of line, form, and mass for the connotative and mood effects indicated by the text; not subtly employed, but strongly etched compositions, moving from one visual relationship to another. This tight control of composition creates a degree of stylization, since its purpose is to play up the dominant aspects of a scene by eliminating the extraneous.

Picturization

Brecht's episodic structure: his interest in focusing attention on the moment for what it contains and not for what it anticipates, for its tension and not for its suspense; his stress on the actor reenacting an event rather than being immersed in it and identifying with it; his striving for social comment in the characters' attitudes toward each other—all point to immaculately rendered, visual statements that picturize the social significance of the immediate text. Each is a study richly expressive, but rendered with a sparsity of means.

Eric Bentley writes:

> When Brecht prepares a play, he works steadily with the composer at the piano, on the whole musical score. When the production is ready, he has hundreds of photographs taken of the action so that he can sit down and examine at leisure all that passes so quickly before the eyes in performance; this, I think, may be called one of the chief ways in which Brecht studies theatre art. He intends each play to be, among other things, a succession of perfectly composed visual images in which every detail counts.

Movement

The carefully composed sequences of visual images, along with strongly delineated gestures, create a choreography not as abstract as pure dance, but highly formal in its own terms in keeping consistent with nature. Brechtian staging deals with the reality of a stage, the reality of actors, and the solidity of things. In this respect, movement, as with composition and picturization, is controlled within this reality, but intensified by a studied attention to form.

Business and Pantomime

Business and pantomime, to enrich character or to establish locale and atmosphere, are used openly with no attempt to create an illusion of the real world. If it becomes necessary to emphasize that the weather is hot, beyond any references in the text, the effect can be stated visually in pantomime or business by the actor through gesture (mopping brow), voice (panting), business (fanning), or movement (plodding). But whatever means selected, the action is deliberate and uncluttered.

Atmosphere and Mood

The epic theatre makes no attempt to simulate atmospheric effects. The intentional bathing of the stage in white light eliminates those elements of atmosphere and environment that normally are intrinsic to the situation in the realistic theatre. There is no masking the fact that events are taking place on a stage. In the spirit of the conventions of the open-air theatres of the past, nighttime can be stated in the text as in a Shakespearean play, or with a placard with the word "night" on it, or with a disc in the shape of a moon.

The use of music is also in keeping with the concept of alienation. Its use is not to intensify mood as in the realistic theatre, but to play in counterpoint to the mood of the moment so as to draw interest by contradiction.

Rhythm

Epic theatre presents a reasoning, contemplative, argumentative form of dialogue, which stimulates the intellect and irritates the emotions through contradictions and interruptions in the flow of events. It implies a highly polished, calculated control. Rhythmically, this means a leisurely pace by which each moment can be savored, consumed, and digested without the pressure of suspense—not that there may not be sequences that cascade into tumultuous frenzy, dynamic clashes of tensions, and palpitating suspense as in the drum beating scene in *Mother Courage*. The overall structure of the play is a narrative to be listened to, an epic account where there is pleasure in each episode and tension, methodically accumulating to a climax.

DIRECTORIAL CONTROLS: PRODUCTION

Ground Plan, Setting, Properties, and Scheme of Production

The frank use of the stage space does not minimize the director's design of the ground plan to express the dramatic values of the play. The scheme of production, far from creating the illusion of an actual place, like a room, simply indicates the locale of the event to be enacted. A wall can represent an entire room without disguising the fact that it is on a stage. Granted this is an illusion; it is not, however, a "make-believe." It also means an economical and selective use of properties—only objects essential to the action are introduced. The properties are real and detailed in texture without implications that a column symbolizes a cathedral, or a chair, a throne room.

Lighting and Costumes

Exposing the stage for what it is means unmasking its instruments. Brecht's insistence on exposing the open space also brought him to use lighting instruments without gelatins so that the action projected its meaning unromanticized by colored lighting or shadow—the meaning of the scene rather than the attempt at mood is all important. Lighting effects, when employed need not have motivation as in the realistic theatre; there is no simulation of rational effects, a spotlight is what it is.

In costuming, detailed attention is given to texture and material to meet the requirements of social identity. The costumes, like the actors, serve to characterize and comment.

CHAPTER ELEVEN

Theatre of the Absurd

The theatre of the absurd encompasses a diversity of styles and basic attitudes, which in some degree project the playwright's denial of reason, logic, purpose, and identity in a world where channels of communication and identification are either non-existent or inconsistent. Its writers dramatize feelings, conditions, and beliefs such as "the futility of the human endeavor," "events in time are insignificant," "man is a stranger in his universe," "a world of shattered beliefs," "the incomprehensibility of life without purpose," and "the fluidity of identity that makes a truth an impossibility." Pinter in a program note for his London production of *The Caretaker* writes of the relativity of truth in these terms: "The basis for verification is understandable, but cannot always be satisfied. There are no hard distinctions between what is true and what is false." We can compare Pinter's dilemma on reality and truth with Pirandello who, however, projected his thesis through logistics in realistic terms.

Stylistically, there is the surrealism of Beckett's *Waiting for Godot*, Albee's *American Dream*, and Genet's *The Balcony*; the romanticism of Frisch's *Don Juan*; the naturalism of Pinter's *The Caretaker*; and the classicism of Ionesco's *The Chairs*—to mention a few examples. Even in these instances the style is only a general indication of the author's manner of expression.

The impression given so far is that the absurdist writers

149

lack focus or consistency. On the contrary, the best of absurdist writing exemplifies aesthetics of high sophistication, where the attempt is to integrate form and subject matter. According to Martin Esslin's *Theatre of the Absurd*, Beckett in *Waiting for Godot* explores a static situation in which:

> The feeling of uncertainty it produces, the ebb and flow of this uncertainty—from the hope of discovering the identity of Godot to its repeated disappointment—are themselves the essence of the play. Instead of linear development as in the conventional play, those of Beckett's present their author's intuition of the human condition by a method that is essentially polyphonic; they confront their audience with an organized structure of statements and images that interpenetrate each other and that must be apprehended in their totality, rather like the different themes in a symphony, which gain meaning by their simultaneous interaction.

The absurdist movement finds its origins in the philosophies of Nietzsche, Kierkegaard, Kafka, and the existentialists; in the metaphysical theories of Artaud; in the relativity of truth as explored by Pirandello; in the "static" drama of Maeterlinck; in the subtextual technique of Chekhov; and in the theatre of improvisation of the *commedia dell' arte*. But unlike the conventional theatre, where the absurdity of the human condition can be argued about and discussed in logical, dramatic terms (as in the plays of Pirandello, Anouilh, Sartre, Camus, Giraudoux, or Williams), the theatre of the absurd presents the absurdity in actual stage images; it concretizes or *objectifies* the idea or thought. Ionesco's idea of the bourgeois man as a status seeker reaches objectification when his satirized man "passes over" into a rhinoceros, the most stupid of animals. In its theatricalities, the absurdist theatre is in direct descendance from the theatre of the *commedia dell' arte*.

The influences of the commedia are in evidence in this movement which seems to scorn clarity in storyline and character behavior, unity and coherence in structure, and rationality in emotional response. Among the chief resources for the improvisations of the commedia actor were the "lazzi"—the italian term for "business," "trick," or "turn" within an event. A "lazzo" was always appropriate to the character but not necessarily to the immediate circumstances. More than not it was introduced as a release from the "eloquence" of talk or for its laugh-provoking quality—Pulcinella staving off his hunger by eating a bee after tearing off its wings is a "lazzo," as is a "gurgling stomach," and an "endearing" fisticuff. Not all "lazzi" are physical. Here is an example of a verbal "lazzo" delivered by Pulcinella:

> There were three hunters: the first without arms, the second without eyes, and the third without legs. The one without arms said, "I shall carry a gun." The one without eyes said, "I shall shoot as soon as I see it." The one without legs said, "And I shall run to take it."

The "lazzo" continues in this vein: the armless, pointing; the eyeless, looking; and the legless, running. Relate this and other "lazzi" to fantastic happenings as Pulcinella turning into a frog for his mock delivery, Pantalone turning into an ass and Franceschina into a tree, and we have a clue to the grotesqueries of the commedia. The playing is made up of absurdities. It respects no bounds to the imagination, bringing its very thoughts to theatrical reality:

Zanni, in his less lucid state, drowns in his own tears of self-pity; Capitano thinks up a storm and scatters his adversaries out of sight; Coviello concentrates on a problem till his brains rattle. Here is *objectification* of a feeling, a thought, and a need.

This startling effect of objectifying a state of mind or condition is a major characteristic of the commedia introduced into the absurdist theatre. If Frisch believes that people stupidly choose to disregard the evil forces at work in society, he dramatizes his theme with a farcical treatment in *Biedermann and the Firebugs*, where two strangers enter Biedermann's house, set up explosives under his hospitality and surveillance, and then proceed to burn down the house. The mother in Kopit's *Oh, Dad, Poor Dad* ceremoniously carries the insistent presence of the dead past in an actual coffin. In Ionesco's *The Tenant*, trivia in the form of furniture accumulates to such mountainous proportions that it immobilizes a tenant in a corner of his room. And in Beckett's *Endgame* the old generation is literally discarded in garbage cans.

Some of the play structuring can also be better appreciated through understanding the nature of commedia acting. The absurdist movement in certain aspects is a theatre of immediacy and emotional contrasts. Heightened emotional moments are pitted against ridiculous reactions. Pinter delights in setting up an amorphous atmosphere of menace, then suddenly puncturing the mood with a naive gurgle of joy followed by a pratfall, as happens in *The Birthday Party*. Edward Bond in *Saved* has the gang scoot the baby carriage one to the other in "fun," then stuns us by having them stone the baby to death. Another writer draws us into a scene by playing on our sentiments with tender strokes of affection, then bashes us into repulsion as one character kicks the other viciously in the groin. These abrupt cataclysmic changes of emotions and attitudes make up the basis of much of the humor in the commedia, though not in the same frame of reference. Quite different from the psychological and physiological follow-through of emotions in subjective acting, commedia acting demands precipitous breaks in emotional projection: you weep, you laugh, and you weep instantaneously, without letting one emotion impinge on the other. The humor of the moment results from this highly etched contrast between opposing emotions. You caress, then suddenly assault, with each action boldly executed unadulterated by the other. It is the immediate juxtaposition of opposing emotions that jolts the audience. The absurdist movement delights in these juxtapositions of emotions and actions.

COMMON CHARACTERISTICS IN THE PLAYS
OF THE THEATRE OF THE ABSURD

Rejection of Logical Causality in Construction

By rejecting logical causality, the absurdist writer integrates formlessness in structure with the formlessness sensed in the human condition. To this extent, he presents his feeling about life by a denial of logic. He creates a sequence of states of thoughts, emotions, and unexplained adventures without sequential follow through. The question is one of "what is happening?" rather than "how will it end?" The total impact creates the coherence, rather than the dependence on a clearly defined story or plot.

Characters without Identity

Many absurdist characters show a fluidity of identity and a lack of personal history. In the plays of Genet, we have a duality of roles, in Pinter the "I–They" seesaw, and in Ionesco, characters who "become at each moment the opposite of themselves." Motivation for character behavior is unfathomable except as the behavior itself sets up conditions that induce certain responses from the audience. The unfixed state of character reflects the view that man is basically inconsistent in his wants and rationality. This ephemeral state of values puts him "out of harmony" with society, which in itself behaves chaotically. The result is that we exist in a world of absurdities.

The absurdist writer, when necessary, will use his characters allegorically, not as abstractly as the allegorical characters of the Mystery plays, but more measurably as a personification of attitudes. The two-nosed fiancee in Ionesco's *Tech or the Submission* and the suburban characters in the plays of Albee are characters of "attitude." The "They" of Pinter is a character that embodies the impersonality of organizational man. The "They" character permeates the thinking and reasons for action or non-action; it enters into our everyday conversation in referring to any segment of society that does not include "us." Thus "They" becomes remote and foreign and therefore fraught with danger. Pinter capitalizes on this to create a devastating sense of menace by the interplay in behavior between the "I" whose state of being is left unanswered and the "They" whose identities remain undefined. In *The Room* the regressive "I" of the wife and husband is pitted against the intrusive "They" of the searchers for a room and the black man waiting in the basement; in *The Dumbwaiter*, the dissatisfied and curious "I" (Gus) is pitted against the acquiescent status quo "They" (Ben).

Elusive Language

A purposeful incoherence exists in language that presents a condition of the world where individuals and institutions are inflicted with an inability to communicate. The torrential flow of nonsensical words from Lucky in *Waiting for Godot*, the babbling sounds of the mute in Ionesco's *The Chairs*, and the talk at cross-purpose in Pinter's *The Caretaker* manifest an integration of form and content that in itself concretizes the idea that in life we no longer are capable of truthfully communicating with each other. Language is only a shell, the meat of its meaning desiccated. The cliché has become a front that prevents us from ever entering into the true thought of an individual who fears intrusion into his private world.

The use of language is "anti-literary" in the sense of being non-descriptive, non-sequential, and free of imageries with ordinary verbal associations. Absurdist characters as in *The Caretaker* have their own way of attacking words. They seize them ravenously, crunching and swallowing the trite and the cliché, then regurgitating them forth in phrasings and fresh associations that assume new meanings. Often the inner sense of rhythm creates a highly sophisticated form of poetry.

The statements made by characters are subject to varying interpretations. As Mick says in *The Caretaker*: "What a strange man you are—everything you speak is open to any number of different interpretations." The absurdist's way is to explore and

154

examine habits, meanings, motivations, criticisms, etc.—to tear off the social veneer and peel away the layers of meaningless attitudinizing. This treatment of language is akin to the subtextual meanings of the Chekhovian dialogue, which is not meant to be taken at face value. Verbal revelation does not necessarily expose the inner thoughts. It is the interpretation of actions and of contradictions in action that leads to the true psychological motivation. Moreover, the actions that contradict what the characters are saying and the variety in handling language—its very obscurity and strangeness—have a fascination in themselves, which stimulate and excite an audience.

Objectification of Ideas

In this one aspect the theatre of the absurd harbors a unique style—the objectification of ideas. As discussed earlier in the chapter, the thesis is not presented in a literary sense. Characters do not explain themselves, nor is the theme developed in the progression of the play. The thesis and the objectification of it are one, or the dramatization of a condition is itself the theme. *Waiting for Godot* explores man's state of stagnant existence in which "nothing happens, nobody comes." The entire play dramatizes this horrendous idea. In Genet's *The Blacks*, the idea of being trapped forever in the status of birth is given effective dramatization not by social revolt as in Hauptmann's naturalistic play *The Weavers* or Toller's expressionistic *Man and the Masses*, but by concretizing the idea through man's escape into games of pretence. The blacks create images of their release from their birthright by putting on white masks.

The plays of writers like Anouilh, Sartre, Camus, and Frisch contain the same basic philosophy of the absurdity of civilized existence, but their works follow a logical structure and are explicit in the development of thesis. They are plays of idea that devastate the logic practiced by our civilization with their own existentialist philosophy. Camus' *Caligula* and Frisch's *Don Juan* are romantic satires—the first a grotesque drama, the second a comedy—that sting the audience's consciousness. Their plays, though intellectually in the spirit of the theatre of the absurd, do not dramatize a condition that creates the thesis. Their method is to create stories and circumstances through which the protagonist shows up the absurdity of conventions, morals, and institutions that govern our life.

Locale and Atmosphere without Orientation

The absurdist plays hold an audience's interest more through intuitive than intellectual understanding. Meaning comes out of the mood generated by the atmosphere, the interplay between characters, and the rhythmic impressions presented by the sequential cumulation of small scenes. The specific locales are microcosms—actions that take place in "a room in a large house" can be our world in the universe. "A country road" in *Waiting for Godot* or "A palace room" in *Tiny Alice* indicates a locale, but since no reference point is given in the text—no orientation—the image left is of a place in limbo.

The device of lack of orientation to the world outside is an important factor in creating an atmosphere of isolation, remoteness, mysticism, or impending doom. Pinter's depiction of the commonplace, lacking orientation, achieves an atmosphere that strengthens his other controls to create a strong sense of approaching menace.

Interplay of Rhythmic Impressions

Unity and coherence in the absurdist play arise out of its totality, but this totality would remain static without the sensitive treatment of rhythm—the life force that integrates all elements into an aesthetic whole. Rhythm is the pulsation that creates final meaning: like poetry and music, it moves the spirit of the audience by its own dynamics. Ultimately, the absurdist writer speaks and performs in the language of the poet and dancer.

DIRECTORIAL CONTROLS: PERFORMANCE

Aesthetic Distance

Since the movement of the theatre of the absurd encompasses diverse styles and creates contradictions in attitudes in the text, we should expect the audience's responses to vary accordingly. The overt machinations of an Ionesco play are fascinating and capture an audience's attention like the performance of a snake charmer, but we cannot say that the audience identifies or gets emotionally involved with either the characters or the situations. Each play may work its own charm, but for the interpreter and performer the task is not only to appreciate and respect the writer's intention, but to arrive at specifics of interpretation through understanding the techniques and work accordingly.

Acting

In absurdist plays the approach to a role, unlike the subjective school of acting, cannot be analyzed out of character motivations and justifications. Objectives are sought from ideas. The ways to depict the actions of characters are unquestionably manifold, but again by understanding the intentions of the particular style of the absurdist writer, the director should be able to decide whether the approach to a role should proceed as discussed under surrealism, under the commedia, or otherwise.

DIRECTORIAL CONTROLS: FUNDAMENTAL ELEMENTS OF DIRECTING

Considerations of style and type guide control in this amorphous theatre. The naturalism of Pinter should be treated as such; so, too, the surrealism of Genet, or the romanticism of Frisch. But there is something more: a phrase or an action cannot be absurd by itself. Absurdity comes out of a comparison with the common acceptance of events or things. What is absurd is so because it is out of norm of expectation, set circumstances, or surroundings. These contradictions must be identified and dramatized.

DIRECTORIAL CONTROLS: PRODUCTION

Scheme of Production

The absurdist theatre permits the unlimited use of stage space within the dramatic justification of the text. A tilting disc platform floating in space can be visually exciting, accentuating atmosphere and mood, provided design is within and illuminates concept. In Pinter's *The Room* or *The Dumbwaiter*, the terror of the commonplace has no meaning unless the locales speak the common denominator to the minutest detail. In many ways this is equivalent to Pinter's use of language, where the clinical attention to commonplace usage in contrast to the circumstances blows up the reality, just as a blown-up photograph of a comb makes us see the article from a new perspective.

CHAPTER TWELVE

Other Styles

Names as environmental theatre, improvisational theatre, or street theatre, and other descriptives as ontological, magic, ridiculous, electric, and living are samples of the avenues to theatrical expression that continue to come in and out of fashion. However, a brief analysis of some of the earlier theatrical adventures in style—impressionism, futurism, constructivism, and happenings—include certain perspectives and influences that add further insights to the study of style.

Impressionism

Impressionism is one of those chameleon-like terms in the complex language of style, that changes its image according to the meaning given it by its user. The term is applied to works that may be basically expressionistic, neoromantic, or realistic; or is used to designate a form or method of artistic expression. Applied promiscuously in the theatre, it generally connotes an inability to recognize the dramatic values of a work which can lead to subsequent misinterpretations and lack of style.

Impressionism used stylistically was first applied to a school of painters that included Monet, Manet, Cezanne, Seurat, and Corot, among many who sought to capture the transient rather than the permanent aspects of nature. These artists portray the *impression* of natural phenomena upon the senses rather than a realistic description of these phenomena. What concerns the theatre worker is the significance of this approach in playrighting and production.

Impressionism in theatre, as in painting, is not a description of reality but the impression that the reality makes on the artist, and his rendering of that impression. He tries to capture nature's momentary, transient qualities rather than its permanent aspects. Mood and atmosphere, therefore, become dominant elements in the impression. Moreover, this mood can be colored by the subjective feelings of the artist to a lesser or greater degree.

If we, as spectators, take what the artist has presented and reverse the process, we should be able to project ourselves, in image and feeling, to the original reality with whatever transient qualities were there. The artist's product—his expression (note carefully) of the impression—evokes the reality. Through the artist's sensitive indications and suggestions, our mind's eye sees what is really not there.

From these definitions we can appreciate the diversified application given to the impressionistic approach. Its dependency on the artist's personal feeling and emotions at the time of execution leans it toward romanticism rather than classicism. Its emphasis on mood and atmospheric touches moves it closer to the neoromanticism of Maeterlinck's mood plays. And looking at the impressionistic approach from the artist's method of selectivity, it is his expression of the dominant aspects of a phenomenon to the exclusion of other details that evokes the entire image. Continuing along this latter view, the part stands for the whole: the realistic throne signifies palace and the power of authority; in Gordon Craig's vocabulary, the light of one candle striking one ascending pillar gives the essence of a church more than the full replica; or, depicting the high points of a man's life in episodes can represent the man's entire life span. Finally, if the artist's feelings color the impression, then the world is seen through the eyes of the individual—it is *his* impression. Following this logic, an action depicted through the subjected state of character as in O'Neill's *Emperor Jones*, would be impressionistic, though it is rightfully considered expressionistic since action and circumstances are seen in frenzied distortion through the state of mind of Jones. The difference is that in the impressionistic manner, as in a Saroyan play, action and circumstances are projected through the personal feeling of the playwright and not the character. While this may be stretching logic, actually in practice the controls and approach to character and scene turn out to be quite different.

Since impressionism has these varying applications, it is essential to distinguish between impressionism as a form or a method and impressionism as a style.

As a form in stage design, a highly selective setting, as the replica of a throne on a level in front of a segment of wall in an otherwise open space, is accepted as representing a palace—the real object stands for the whole. This is a realistic symbol that signifies palace. Within this frame of reference, Sherwood's *Abe Lincoln in Illinois* and Housman's *Victoria Regina*, structured in episodes realistically depicting high points in the protagonist's life, give insight into the entire existence of the individual. Again, carefully selected portions are made to represent the whole. This method of design and writing, though called impressionistic in form, is actually not wholly within the spirit of impressionism as, for example, Craig's design of the candle and pillar mentioned earlier. Craig's design is a symbol of the whole which, through mood and atmosphere, creates the essence of church or, more significantly, the spiritual quality of religion. This also holds true for H. R. Lenormand's *The Failures* and Peter Shaffer's *Amadeus* which, though structurally similar in form to *Abe Lincoln in Illinois* and *Victoria Regina*, also evoke dimensions and implications in human values not by documenting events, but through use of moods and atmospheres in relating the struggles and confrontations.

Tennessee Williams, in his introduction to *The Glass Menagerie*, writes:

Everyone should know nowadays the unimportance of the photographic in art; that truth, life, or reality is an organic thing which the poetic imagination can represent or suggest, in essence, only through transformation, through changing into other forms than those which were merely present in appearance.

The statement contains the essential feeling for impressionism as exemplified in *The Glass Menagerie*, as well as in his *Streetcar Named Desire*, *Summer and Smoke*, and *Suddenly Last Summer*.

Also consistent in the impressionistic style are the plays of William Saroyan which capture the totality of existence—not by penetrating to the center of the matter, but by catching life's events in fragments and diffusion of images. His *Time of Your Life*, *My Heart's in the Highlands*, and *Cave Dwellers* are good examples. Saroyan creates impressions rather than depict actions; he evokes rather than explains; he listens to feelings and rejects reason; he paints atmospheres with imageries; he engenders a mood of existence without detailing necessities of living—and finally, he underscores everything with his own personal feeling for the oneness of man and the fundamental goodness in mankind.

The snatches of reality, sentimentalized or otherwise, imply more than what is present in the action. This means that as an audience we fill in the picture through our own knowledge of life's events. Directorially, it is equivalent to leading up to a picturized relationship but, before completing the follow-through of the action, fading the lights on it and leaving the audience to complete the scene in its own vision.

The principle of not overdetailing also holds true in rendering business and pantomime. The horn in *My Heart's in the Highlands*, the toy carousel in *Time of Your Life*, and the menagerie in *The Glass Menagerie* are instruments that the playwright has introduced to accentuate the color, mood, or atmosphere of a scene, rather than to enrich character. Any detailing in their use would bring attention to the performer, thereby diffusing their effectiveness otherwise.

In acting, character must be strengthened and vitalized as

in neoromanticism. The tendency to melt into the pervading mood and atmosphere should be avoided. Instead, when necessary, mood should be produced by emphasizing the connotative values of composition, movement, and rhythm.

Futurism

Like the Dadaists, the Futurists can be called anarchists who revolted against the past and repudiated its art, culture, and religion. They came into prominence during the first decade of the twentieth century, when a rebel group of Italian painters and sculptors formulated their theories under the leadership of Filippo Tommaso Marinetti, whose article "Foundation and Manifesto of Futurism" in the magazine Figaro in 1909 became the guide of this post-impressionist group. Later, Marinetti writes that "a play must be technical, dynamic, simultaneous, autonomous, alogical and unreal." In Furutist terms, life is not lived in a predetermined form but in continual impressions that are disjointed and unrelated.

These pronouncements make little sense unless we go behind the descriptions to the state of mind of these radicals, who set out intentionally to invent something new in art. They saw life as dynamic and tried to capture experience in terms of its dynamics: the truth of an object rests in its inner rhythmic force, expressed through movement in contention with its surrounding lines and planes. Carried over into sculpture, the spectator senses the dynamics of the subject and not the subject itself. Arp, in his sculpture *Bird in Flight*, renders the dynamics of a bird in flight rather than the object, bird. In painting, in what is now accomplished with action photography, the dynamics of a dog walking are rendered by a flurry of legs. Or in abstract paintings, more akin to expressionism, the spectator is drawn to the center of the picture with the subject matter in violent action around him. But whatever the intention, symbolic or otherwise, the final effect in the best futuristic art is decorative rather than expressionistic.

From another point of view, the Futurists saw life as fleeting and energized, never in controllable form but in a series of disconnected impressions. The verisimilitude of life can be captured only by depicting the "simultaneity" of its events. Life consists of many events happening simultaneously without sequence or logic. In structuring a play, this means the representation of several events at the same time or in quick succession, even those separated in time and space. In one of the Futurist productions, the setting was a facade of several open cubicles mounted vertically in three levels. In each a different realistic scene was in action with the overall dynamics and lighting controlled to shift emphasis from one cubicle to another.

Marinetti's brief excursion into playwriting resulted in a theatre of curiosity rather than one with any semblance to humanity. His *Simultanina* attempts to dramatize the changing appearance of a woman as she is viewed by each of her lovers. This concept has been carried into multifaceted portrayals of character. In a production of *Hamlet*, the role of Hamlet was enacted by three actors, each portraying certain facets of character. Other Marinetti mini-sketches are strange diversions and grotesqueries. In one, furniture talks to give a sense of its human inhabitants; in another, the parade and intermingling of legs of people seen behind a partially raised curtain indicate a sense of character, attitudes, and circumstances by means of movement and variety of rhythms. These are experiments that found further fruition in the absurdist movement.

The Futurists' love for the dynamics of life brought them into a kinesthetic affinity with the machine, which gave them the inspiration for their abstract and mechanistic designs. The machine and the use of materials produced by man exemplified the spirit of their age. In stage design, this feeling for the heartbeat and movement of machinery was transposed into atmospheric scenery that moved in space—an interplay of planes, lines, forms, lights, sound, and color, that captures the panorama of life by its myriad pictures. Here was the inspiration for new methods that were to have their influence on later designers and directors, as can be seen particularly in the contemporary musicals.

The inner dynamics and "simultaneity" created new schemes of production that flourished in the constructivist theatre, the living newspaper, and epic drama productions. Multiple scenes (simultaneous or in quick succession), dynamic use of scenery, direct stimulation of audience, streamlined design, psychedelic lighting, and flash videos are some of the latter outgrowths of this rebellion against the traditional theatre of illusion.

Directorially, the technical application of the fundamentals of directing holds special significance, at least in the Futurist playlets and multiscene experiments. However, for the theatre, the value of the Futurist movement rests more in its service as a catalyst to theatrical development than in its own endeavors.

Constructivism

The polarity in the anti-realistic movement can be found by contrasting the expressionistic and constructivistic attitudes toward the machine as a symbol of its age: the former propagandized on the brutal horror of the machine, while the latter glorified it. Vsevold Meyerhold, political revolutionary and outspoken proponent, saw in the machine the essence of a new future emanating from technological and biological development—an embodiment of the movement and sounds of the time; a constructive device. He felt that the theatre needed to be revitalized, since he perceived it as a means to an end and not an end in itself. Meyerhold believed in the *kinesthetic*, that is, the physical communication between actor and audience, so that the audience becomes a participant in the action. To this end, he stripped the stage of its illusionistic paraphernalia, exposing walls and technical instruments. In the space he engineered a grouping of platforms, steps, ramps, wheels, gratings, and so on, to allow unhampered movement of the actors.

The principle of mechanistic display was also followed in the training of actors, who by understanding the mechanics of the body, used it effectively for any physical demands. After grasping his part intellectually, the actor was required to translate it into physical terms. This physical integration between the functions of setting, body, and intellect became the ultimate aim of the actor's training in "biomechanics," Meyerhold's word for his program.

This mobile symbolism of constructivism was inextricably bound up with the conceptual aspects of presentation. Socially, it embodies the spirit of collectivism as opposed to individualism, in the belief that communal understanding can be achieved only through the externals of behavior. The inner life is too variable, too self-serving, ever to serve as the center for universal brotherhood. Even the setting is an abstraction of the meaning, attitude, and point of view in the play. Every part serves a purpose and is built out of the specific demands of the basic situations. The unique feature of this style is audience stimulation; the purpose being to agitate the audience through *direct stimulation*—the kinesthetic aspect of constructivism. The audience is moved by sensational means, that is, you *are* surprised, rather than being surprised in empathic response to a character.

DEMONSTRATION

A character is swaying on a swing, positioned high above the stage floor. A second character enters, receives a letter, reads it, and registers surprise. At this instant, the character swinging falls unexpectedly. The audience is surprised by this unexpected incident; therefore, the audience is surprised, rather than being surprised because of any empathic response to the character reading the letter.

This sensationalism in introducing the unexpected or incongruous element to sustain the audience's interest and stimulate it into participation is an important aspect of constructivism. Communication is through direct contact, not empathy. The audience is assaulted. Actors spill out and speak directly to the people, inspiring them to participate and react. In Meyerhold's activist theatre, the audience was known to march out with the actors, joining them in their communistic protestations. The American counterpart to this form of agitprop theatre (agitation and propaganda) is the Group Theatre's production of Odet's *Waiting for Lefty* and other participatory productions by groups like La Mama, though many of these have moved into other aspects of kinetic and aural interplay. Environmental and street theatre are also part of this action theatre of audience participation.

In practice, constructivism is a manner of staging. Plays, particularly the classics as directed by Meyerhold, are adapted to the conceptual demands of the director. The challenge lies in the search for the sensational—the unexpected or incongruous action that will directly stimulate the emotions of the spectator.

DEMONSTRATION

An anti-war production. The action on stage is the suppression of members of a group of dissenters. At a crucial moment in the onstage action, the doors of the auditorium burst open as armed militia in recognizable uniforms rush in. Several run up on stage and fire a warning. Others hold guns on the audience as the leader of the militia speaks of the civil uprising outside. Sporadic gunshots are heard outside as he speaks. Meanwhile, other militia pass along the aisles demanding the surrender of hidden arms and narcotics.

The disadvantage with this kind of theatre is that it wears thin with subsequent performances when more members of the audience are in the know. Also, in "activist" theatre there is a self-conscious factor in members of the audience to contend with in these confrontations, which can increase rather than reduce aesthetic distance.

Happenings

A popular and in many ways an elitist entertainment phenomenon of the late fifties and early sixties was the experimentation in combining improvisations with "chance" happenings, either planned or inspired by the exigencies of the moment. The Happening is a one-time performance that uses a variety of elements (common and perishable properties, physical antics, pantomime, dance, readings, music, film, projections, lighting and sound effects, bizarre costuming and makeup, set pieces, etc.), singly and otherwise, taking place in a natural or artificially constructed environment, and, in circumstances without characterization, plot, beginnings, or resolution. Basic to the Happening is that the audience and event fuse into one.

Happenings began as an extension of the work of action painters, joined by sculptors and musicians with roots in the experiments of Futurists, Dadaists, Constructivists, and Surrealists. To these could be added the panorama of mimes, circus, masques, and so on, in a long procession of people's theatre. The events that make up a Happening are limitless.

DEMONSTRATION

A performance can be a single event: in a vast echoing hall filled with towering museum pieces, a nude dancer majestically struts down a fifty-yard red carpet runner, stops, then nonchalantly disappears into the shadows.

Or it can be a mingling of occurrences in some loft: people mill around breathing foul or perfumed air, bumping their way through obstructions and falling objects with bells ringing and shapes protruding from below and above; words, sensible and nonsensical, undulate from all corners; projected images of junk foods crawl over people and walls. Stimulated by this melee, the participants laugh and jostle, contributing their own witty or cliché comments. All react and share in an experience that can never be repeated and which leaves each individual with his own private perception.

Or it can be a structured event: the audience is seated; the house lights partially dim; the audience waits in silence. A formally dressed man enters and walks gracefully to a position behind a long table on the platform. He reaches down and comes up with a pair of white gloves, which he places by him; he reaches down again and comes up with several pairs of white gloves, which he places in pairs along the front edge of the long table; he reaches down a third time and brings up several long, tapered white candles, which he places above each pair of white gloves. He holds position for a moment, then points to several members in the audience and beckons them to come forward. He asks each to stand in front of a pair of gloves, their backs to the audience. He puts on his white gloves and signals the others to do the same; he lights his candle with a lighter which he takes out of his pocket; with his lighted candle, he lights those held by the others. He signals them to turn and face the audience, each holding up his lighted candle; then he comes forward from behind the table and takes position in front of the group, facing them. Signaling the two end people, he has them come forward and stand before him as a couple. He raises his candle high and starts humming in a low monotone, nodding to the others to do the same; all hum. He signals the others to follow in couples behind the first pair; the house lights go out, leaving only the candlelight. He moves forward very slowly and proceeds down the center aisle as the others follow in couples. All reach the rear of the auditorium. Silence. The house lights come up abruptly.

Happenings have been extended to include demonstrations of any sort, "sit-ins" and "be-ins," and fun and games. Many resent the nomenclature "art" for what to them is a hodgepodge of nonsensical accidents. For others it is an experience to be shared and relished, allowing them release without censure and freedom for spontaneity of expression. The permissiveness of Happenings caters to each participant's conceit of creativity. On the other hand, the Happening nurtured out of artistry can have a frame of reference: there can be selectivity, with limits set as to the number of elements and their nature; as a concept, it allows the work to develop by "chance" no different from the inspiration of the artist absorbed in the process of the work. Moreover, for the believers, the element of "chance" brings to the event the excitement of risk and anticipation without penalty of failure. For these people, Happenings exist for their own sake, ephemeral and without pretensions.

Closing Statement

As in other areas of our activities, ventures into new ways of theatrical expression continue from generation to generation, fascinating audiences with innovative presentations. Some may be reminiscent of earlier cycles as the neo-dadaism, performed in structured pictorial macabre happenings; others offer exciting potpourri theatricals of different cultures, making use of Shakespearean texts performed in Kabuki ritualistic stylization; and still others take off on older fads dressed in new disguises, performing the futurist concept of "simultaneity" in multiple areas, but secretive one from the other. Whatever the venture, the basic attitude, the purpose, the essential elements of the work, the manner of expression, the conventions or anti-conventions that are operative, the techniques of acting, the mechanics of staging, the scheme of production, and the approach taken in bringing the effort to performance level, all these are involved to a lesser or greater degree whether by choice or accident, or whether meaningful or otherwise.

The focus of this study has been to offer some assistance to the beginning director in developing a clearer understanding of the working parts of a play and the considerations involved in this most sensitive process of selection and control.

Bibliography

Major quotations and play selections

Bentley, Eric. *German Stagecraft Today*. Kenyon Review, Vol. XI, No. 4.

Brecht, Bertolt. *Brecht on Theatre*. Edited and translated by John Willet. New York: Hill & Wang, 1964.

Cheney, Sheldon. *The Theatre*. New York: David McKay Co., 1972.

Esslin, Martin. *The Theatre of the Absurd*. New York: Anchor Books, 1969.

Funke, Lewis and Booth, John E. *Actors Talk about Acting*. New York: Random House, 1961.

Guiness, Alec. An interview in *Show*. December, 1964.

Maeterlinck, Maurice. *Pelleas and Melisande*. Translated by Richard Hovey. New York: Dodd, Mead & Co., 1911.

Maeterlinck, Maurice. *The Treasure of the Humble*. Translated by Alfred Sutro. New York: Dodd, Mead & Co., 1897.

Miller, Arthur. *A View from the Bridge*. New York: The Viking Press, 1960.

Rice, Elmer. *The Adding Machine*. New York: Doubleday, Doran & Co., 1923.

Shaw, G. B. *Shaw on Theatre*. Edited by E. J. West. New York: Hill & Wang, 1958.

Williams, Tennessee. Foreword to *The Glass Menagerie*. New York: Random House, 1945.

Index

Acting: classicism, 96–97; comedy, 23–24; epic realism, 143–145; expressionism, 124–125; farce, 39—40; melodrama, 67–68; naturalism, 75–78; romanticism, 109–110; selective realism, 85–86; surrealism, 135; theatre of the absurd, 157; tragedy, 48–50

Adding Machine, The, selection from, 125–127

Aesthetic distance: classicism, 96; epic realism, 142–143; expressionism, 124; naturalism, 75; romanticism, 108–109; surrealism, 134–135; theatre of the absurd, 157

Approach to rehearsal, xviii–xix

Arsenic and Old Lace, 64

As You Like It, xviii

Atmosphere: classicism, 99; comedy, 19–20; epic realism, 147; farce, 37; naturalism, 81–82; romanticism, 111; theatre of the absurd, 156; tragedy, 48–50

Balcony, The, 136

Biedermann and the Firebug, 151–152

Black comedy, 9

Business, xx; classicism, 99; comedy, 17–19; epic realism, 146–147; farce, 36–39; naturalism, 80–81; romanticism, 111; tragedy, 48

Caligula, 57

Caretaker, The, 154–155

Casting: comedy, 28–29; farce, 40–41; melodrama, 68; serious plays, 52–53

Catharsis, 43–44

Caucasian Chalk Circle, The, 141–142

Charley's Aunt, 33–34

Cherry Orchard, The, 22–23, 51, 74, 75–77, 81, 87–88; selection from, 75–77

Classicism, 90–101

Comedy, 3–29

Comedy of idea, 9

Comedy of manners, 7–8

Commedia dell' arte, 144, 150–152

Composition, xix; classicism, 97; comedy, 16; epic realism, 145; farce, 34–35; naturalism, 78; romanticism, 110; tragedy, 46

"conceptual awareness," 93–94

Connotative values, xvii

Constructivism, 165–167

Cyrano de Bergerac, 117

Doctor in Spite of Himself, The, 32

Economy of means, 49–50

175

Elements of a play, xv
Endgame, 136
Epic realism, 138–148
Expressionism, 118–129

Farce, 30–42
Fundamental design, xvii, 50–51, 127–128
Fundamental elements of directing, xix–xxi
Futurism, 163–165

Gags, 36–37
Genre, xiv
"gestural acting," 143–145
Glass Menagerie, The, 161–162
Good Woman of Setzuan, The, 140

Happenings, 168–170
High comedy, 6

Importance of Being Earnest, The, 14
Impressionism, 159–163
Incongruity, 11–12
Intensification and the tragic tone, 48–49
Jim Dandy, 136
Journey's End, 119–120

Laugh lines, 24–28
"lazzi," 151

Melodrama, 54–58
Melodrama of idea, 56–57
Mood: classicism, 99; comedy, 19–20; epic realism, 147; farce, 37; naturalism, 81–82; romanticism, 111; tragedy, 48–50
Movement, xx; classicism, 98–99; comedy, 17; epic realism, 146; farce, 35–36, 38–39; naturalism, 79–80; romanticism, 111; tragedy, 47–48

Mystery and murder melodramas, 55–56, 64–65

Naturalism, 71–89; compared with selective realism, 83–89
Neoclassicism, 101–103
Neoromanticism, 112–117; selection from Pelleas and Melisande, 114–116; "static drama," 113
No Exit, 57

Objectification, 151–152, 155–156
Oedipus Rex, 98–99
Othello, 47–48

Pace, 20–21, 37
Pantomime, xx; classicism, 99; epic realism, 146–147; naturalism, 80–81; romanticism, 111
Pelleas and Melisande, selection from, 114–116
Period conventions, xvii
Petrified Forest, 56
Picturization, xx; classicism, 97; comedy, 16; epic realism, 145–146; farce, 35; naturalism, 79; romanticism, 110–111; tragedy, 46
Plant, the, 64
"playing the game," 14–15
Psychological melodrama, 56
Purpose, xiv–xv

Realism, 83–89
Rehearsals: comedy, 29; farce, 41–42; serious plays, 53
Relief scenes, 52, 64
Right You Are, 87–88
Romanticism, 104–112
Rhythm, xxi; classicism, 99–100; comedy, 20–21; epic realism, 147; farce, 37; naturalism, 82; romanticism, 112; tragedy, 48–49

Satiric comedy, 8–9
Scheme of production, xvii–xviii; classicism, 100–101; epic realism, 148; expressionism, 128–129; futurism, 165; naturalism, 83; romanticism, 112; theatre of the absurd, 158
Selective realism, 83–89; compared with naturalism, 84–89
Sentimental comedy, 5–6; compared to melodramatic, 65–68
"shockers," 63–64
"simultaneity," 164–165
Situation comedy, 5
Situation melodrama, 55
"static drama," 113
Style, xiii, xv–xvi, 68–170
Stylization, 125–127
Surrealism, 130–137
Suspense scenes, 61–64

Teasers, 61–63
Tempo, 20–21, 37
Theatre of the absurd, 149–158
Theatrical conventions, xvi
Three Men on a Horse, 35
Tragedy, 43–53
Twelfth Night, 10, 38–39, 105
Type of play, xiv, 1–68

View from the Bridge, A, 91–93; selection from, 91–92
Visit, The, 128–129

Waiting for Godot, 150
Winterset, 107